WITHDRAWN

The Common Market and World Agriculture

Francis Knox

The Praeger Special Studies program—
utilizing the most modern and efficient book
production techniques and a selective
worldwide distribution network—makes
available to the academic, government, and
business communities significant, timely
research in U.S. and international economic, social, and political development.

The Common Market and World Agriculture

Trade Patterns in Temperate-Zone Foodstuffs

PRAEGER SPECIAL STUDIES IN INTERNATIONAL ECONOMICS AND DEVELOPMENT

Praeger Publishers   New York   Washington   London

PRAEGER PUBLISHERS

111 Fourth Avenue, New York, N.Y. 10003, U.S.A.

5, Cromwell Place, London S.W.7, England

Published in the United States of America in 1972
by Praeger Publishers, Inc.

© 1972 by Praeger Publishers, Inc.

Library of Congress Catalog Card Number: 74-170273

Printed in the United States of America

Whatever the final outcome of the third series of negotiations between Great Britain and the Common Market countries, it is likely that, during the first half of the 1970's, there will be a radical re-examination of the existing structure of international trade in agricultural goods. The position of the British Commonwealth food-exporting countries is one of the main points at issue in the negotiations, and, if Great Britain joins the Common Market, it is unlikely that the problems of these nations can be solved without bringing in other food-exporting and importing countries.

The development of the Common Market's Common Agricultural Policy during the 1960's has had a serious effect on some food-exporting countries, especially Denmark. The interest of the United States, as a major food-exporting country, in this problem will probably result in much greater attention being paid to agriculture in future negotiations in the General Agreement on Tariffs and Trade (GATT). In addition, since GATT has made substantial progress in reducing tariffs on industrial products, the next item on its agenda is likely to be nontariff barriers to international trade, one of the most important of which is the various forms of government support to agriculture. It is therefore urgent to be aware of recent trends in international trade and to try to establish criteria for action.

In Chapter 1, the effects of "irrational" trends in international trade are discussed. The contribution of the Common Market farm policy to these trends is assessed in Chapter 2. Two major influences on agricultural policy in Great Britain—the European Free Trade Association and the balance-of-payments problem—are the subjects of Chapters 3 and 4. Chapter 4 specifically deals with the cost-of-living and balance-of-payments problems facing Great Britain if it joins the Common Market, and, although no attempt is made to quantify the disadvantages to Great Britain of adopting the Common Agricultural Policy (these disadvantages depend fundamentally on the level of producer prices in the enlarged Common Market, which will not be known for some years after the start of the transition period), proposals are made for mitigating some of the adverse effects.

In Chapter 5, the need for objective and rational criteria in existing and proposed international commodity agreements is stressed.

Chapter 6 puts forth the argument that the same criteria that should be used as a measure of agricultural protection in international negotiations and as a criteria for allocation of production or export shares in international agreements—that is, the difference between internal producer prices and world market prices—is also the best available measure of efficiency in national agricultural comparisons. Finally, the prospects and preconditions of a wider reform in international trade in agriculture are touched on in Chapter 7.

This book deals only with temperate-zone agriculture. The problems of tropical producers (those offering such products as coffee, tea, and cocoa) are not dealt with, nor are the problems of producers of agricultural products used as industrial raw materials, such as tobacco, cotton, and wool. The issues raised for countries producing these products by the possibility of British entry into the Common Market and by the development of Common Market policies to date are less acute than those raised for temperate-zone agricultural countries, since there is less direct competition between European and non-European producers. Sugar could have been included, since it is both a temperate-zone (beet) and tropical (cane sugar) product; however, it has been left out becuase the problems involved are rather different and have already been dealt with elsewhere.* Totals in the tables below are not always the sum of the items given, because of the rounding off of figures; also, a dash means nil or negligible; and n. a. means not available.

---

*See, for example, articles by F. G. Sturrock and A. Tasker in National Westminister Bank Quarterly Review (August, 1969, and February, 1970); and David Jones, "The Commonwealth Sugar Industry and the European Economic Community," Bulletin of the Oxford Institute of Statistics, XXIX, 3 (August, 1967), 211-32.

LIST OF TABLES

LIST OF ABREVIATIONS

CAP	Common Agricultural Policy
CEC	Commonwealth Economic Committee
c.i.f.	cost, insurance, and freight
cwt.	hundredweight
ECE	Economic Commission for Europe
EDC	Economic Development Committee
EEC	European Economic Community
EFTA	European Free Trade Association
FAO	Food and Agriculture Organization
FEOGA	Fonds Europeens d'Orientation et de Garantie Agricole
GATT	General Agreement on Tariffs and Trade
GNP	gross national product
HMSO	Her Majesty's Stationery Office
IFAP	International Federation of Agricultural Producers
ITO	International Trade Organization
IWA	International Wheat Agreement
OECD	Organization for Economic Cooperation and Development
SITC	Standard International Trade Classification
UNCTAD	United Nations Conference on Trade and Development
VAT	value-added tax
—	in tables, signifies "nil" or "negligible"

n. a.   in tables, signifies "not available"

£, s., d.   pound, shilling, pence (All prices quoted in the book are
            in pre-decimal British currency.)

The Common Market and World Agriculture

Probably more so than with manufacturing and with tropical foodstuffs, it is possible to classify countries producing one main group of temperate-zone agricultural products—cereals, meat, and dairy products—into two distinct categories—high-cost and low-cost producers. This clear-cut distinction does not apply to the second main group of temperate-zone foods—fruit and vegetables—where southern Europe, which is a high-cost producer of other temperate-zone foods, has climatic advantages; nor does it apply to the third group—fishing the forest products. For cereals, meat, and dairy products, the countries that are high-cost producers are mainly those of continental Western Europe, whereas those that are low-cost producers are non-European.

The reasons for this situation are rooted more in history than in geography and economics and will not be discussed here.[1] Regarding cereals, however, there are advantages in large farms comparable to the economies of scale obtained by large firms in manufacturing—hence, the competitive advantage of Australia, Canada, the United States, and Argentina, where settlement has been fairly recent and rural population pressure has not led to small farms.

The main reason for the generally greater efficiency of British agriculture compared with that of continental Western Europe in producing the three main groups of temperate foodstuffs is to be found in the law of primogeniture and of entail (whereby a son who inherited an estate was merely a life tenant and could not sell the estate). In France, in contrast, the French Revolution

made compulsory the already widespread practice of dividing property equally. The Code Napoléon modified

the rule a little: if there was only one child, the father
could bequeath half his property as he wished, if there
were two children he could bequeath freely of one-third;
and if there were three or more the fraction was a quarter.
The rest must be equally divided. 2

Similar laws applied in most other continental Western European
countries—hence, the successive subdivision of farms, which has
persisted to the present, as evidenced by the existence of the medieval
three-field system in some parts of Europe. This practice also led
to farms that were too small and those in which the operator spent a
large part of his working time traveling between various parts of his
farm. (The typical West German farmer lives in a village and travels
daily to his work, whereas the typical British farmhouse is located
in the center of the farm.)

For various reasons, the enclosure movement, which brought
about a rationalization of British agriculture in the late eighteenth
and early nineteenth centuries, made little headway on the European
continent until much late, and even than it was on a smaller scale.
Finally, the absence of a large and rapidly growing manufacturing
sector in many parts of Western Europe before World War II
meant that there was no alternative employment for workers who
wished to leave the land. With the single exception of Denmark (and,
to a lesser extent, the Netherlands), the countries of continental
Europe are still suffering from this historical legacy.*

Since around 1955, however, a trend has emerged, largely due
to the formation of the European Economic Community (EEC) —that
is, the Common Market—for the countries of Western Europe that
are high-cost producers of agricultural products to expand their
exports, at the expense of the non-European countries that are low-
cost producers and of Denmark. In a few cases, this has led to an
absolute decline in the exports of the low-cost producers; in more
cases, though, it has led only to stagnation in the quantity and value
of the exports of the low-cost producers; and, in other cases, although
their exports have continued to grow, they have done so more slowly
than have the exports of the high-cost producers, so that their share
of the world market has fallen. This trend may be considerably
accentuated if Great Britain joins the Common Market, because of
its importance as a food importer.

---

*East Germany, where the large landowners were powerful,
also avoided the subdivision and fragmentation of farms.

All the countries that are low-cost producers of agricultural products—Denmark, Ireland, Australia, New Zealand, South Africa, South America, the United States, and Canada—have been affected by this trend. It is probably accurate to include some of the Eastern European countries—Poland, Yugoslavia, and East Germany—in the category of low-cost producers, although the nature of prices and exchange rates in Soviet economies makes it very difficult to compare prices.

Exports from Eastern European countries have also been affected by the Common Market, with the exception of East Germany, whose food exports are not subject to EEC levies. Although Denmark and Ireland will almost certainly join the Common Market if Great Britain does and will therefore benefit from higher producer prices and probably a larger sales volume, all the low-cost producers are major exporters to Great Britain and all will be affected—much more than by the evolution of the Common Agricultural Policy (CAP) before Great Britain's accession.

The effects of agricultural protection on international trade were noted in 1958 in the Haberler Report, put out by the General Agreement on Tariffs and Trade (GATT), although this was mainly concerned with the problems of underdeveloped countries. [3] The Haberler Report points out (in paragraph 46) that

> Since in North America and Western Europe as a whole net imports of agricultural products represent the relatively narrow margin by which their large domestic consumption exceeds their large, but not quite so large, domestic production, a relatively small restraint on domestic production or stimulus to domestic consumption could lead to a large percentage increase in their net imports. For this reason much could be achieved by some moderate change in the direction of the agricultural policies of the highly industrialised countries.

The Report also commented (in paragraph 58) that

> the agricultural arrangements in the EEC will be of special importance for the prospects of outside producers of primary products. The Treaty of Rome does not lay down in detail how the agricultural marketing arrangements and the long-term contracts of the EEC will be applied; but it is important that they should not be applied so as to reduce the European demand for imported agricultural products.

Since 1958, there has probably been an increase in the degree
of agricultural protection in the EEC as a result of the development
of the CAP. (See Chapter 2.) There has also been a deliberate effort
to increase domestic agricultural output in the United Kingdom because
of balance-of-payments difficulties. (See Chapter 4.) Although U.S.
policies are not considered in this book, there may have been an
increase in agricultural protection there.

The more obvious effects of these policies have been on the
exports and national income of the low-cost food producing countries
and on the cost of living in the importing countries, but the more
fundamental effects may be assumed to be a misallocation of economic
resources and a lower standard of living than would otherwise be the
case both in the importing and the exporting countries. Since cereals,
meat, and dairy products are a large proportion of total world trade
in foodstuffs, the effects on resource allocation and standards of living
must be far-reaching, although there is no way in which they can be
satisfactorily quantified.

Table 1 summarizes data on the producer prices of some of the
most important and representative temperate-zone agricultural products in some of the main exporting countries. The criterion of selec-
tion of countries, apart from being quoted by the Food and Agriculture
Organization (FAO), is merely that the country concerned is an important exporter.

Wheat is the most important of temperate-zone cereal products
in terms of quantities entering international trade, and its price is of
basic importance to cereal prices generally, although wheat is used
mainly for human consumption, whereas coarse grains, of which the
most important is barley, are used mainly for livestock feeding.
Thus, there is some divergence between wheat and barley prices (and
some difference in countries ranked according to the producer prices
of wheat and barley). Maize is also very important as an animal
foodstuff, but it is exported mainly by the United States.

As can be seen from Table 1, the producer price of wheat in
Italy and West Germany is nearly three times that in Argentina; in
France, Ireland, the Netherlands, and Sweden, it is lower but still
more than twice the price in Argentina; in the United Kingdom, it is
less than double the Argentinian price; and, in the United States, it
is only 40 per cent higher than the Argentinian price.

If one allows for cost of transport and if Western Europe (including the United Kingdom is regarded as the relevant consuming center,

TABLE 1

Producer Prices of Selected Agricultural Products, 1965-69 (Average Inclusive)
(U.S. Cents per Kg.)

Wheat		Barley		Maize		Beef Cattle (live weight)		Pigs (slaughter weight)	
Country	Price	Country	Price	Country	Price	Country	Price	Country	Price
Argentina	3.7	West Germany	3.4	Argentina	3.4	Belgium	77.9	Canada	66.3
Belgium	9.5	Brewing barley	9.9	Italy	8.3	West Germany	70.8	Denmark	64.9
		Fodder barley	9.0						
Canada	6.1	Japan	15.1	United States	4.5	Italy	76.2	New Zealand	64.9
France	8.4	United Kingdom	6.3	Yugoslavia	5.1	Netherlands	66.9	United Kingdom	68.1
West Germany	10.0	United States	4.4			United States	48.4		
Ireland	8.5								
Italy	10.5								
Japan	14.6								
Netherlands	9.8								
Sweden	9.8								
United Kingdom	6.7								
United	5.1								

Poultry, Chicks (live weight)		Butter		Cheese		Eggs	
Country	Price	Country	Price	Country	Price	Country	Price
Canada		Australia	100	Australia	61.9	Belgium	59.6
Fowls (over 6 lb.)	33.8	Belgium	189	Denmark	54.0	Denmark	51.9
Chickens (under 5lb.)	40.8	Denmark	102	West Germany	120.9	Italy	68.2
West Germany	49.2	Ireland	106	Italy		Netherlands	54.6
Italy		Netherlands	154	Parmesan (1 yr. old, first quality, Reggio Emilia)	231.7	United Kingdom (4-yr. average, 1965-68)	54.4
Fowls	116.7	Sweden	123	Sheep's cheese (first class, Viterbo)	195.1		
Chickens (medium)	121.0	Switzerland	289				
United States				Netherlands	83.0		
Farm Chickens	19.2						
Commercial broilers	31.9			Switzerland	135.7		
Denmark							
Fowls (first class)	32.0						
Chickens (extra class)	44.2						

Source: FAO, Production Yearbook, 1969 (Rome, 1970); and FAO, Monthly Bulletin of Agricultural Economics and Statistics (Rome, monthly publication).

Argentina, Canada, the United Kingdom, and the United States are low-cost wheat-producing countries (as well as Australia, not included in the FAO figures); Ireland and France are medium-cost producers; and Belgium, West Germany, Italy, and the Netherlands are clearly uncompetitive. In a free (and/or rational) market, wheat production in the four latter countries would be considerably less than at present, and the resources used in wheat production would be devoted either to some other agricultural product or (more probably) to nonagricultural use.

If one uses FAO figures together with figures collated by the International Federation of Agricultural Producers (IFAP, see Table 2), it seems that Denmark, Ireland, and the United Kingdom (as well as the United States) are low-cost producers of barley; France is a medium-cost producer; and the other Western European countries are high-cost producers.

According to the FAO figures, the producer price of beef cattle in West Germany, Italy, and Belgium-Luxembourg is some 50 per cent higher than in the USA; and, in the Netherlands, only slightly less than that. Within the European countries, the IFAP figures again show Denmark, Ireland, and (to a lesser extent) the United Kingdom as low-cost producers and the other Western European countries as high-cost producers. A similar picture emerges for pigmeat, though the differences between low-cost and high-cost producers in Western Europe are less than for other products. Poultry prices are twice as high in West Germany as in the United States, and more than twice as high in Italy as in West Germany.

In Table 3, the IFAP figures for Western European countries are expressed as a percentage of Danish producer prices. In this and the preceding tables, an average has been taken of the years 1965/66-1968/69 to avoid the problem of year-to-year fluctuations and also to reduce the problem of converting to a common (dollar) unit following the British devaluation of 1967. In the EEC, there has been a convergence of prices during these years as the CAP has become fully effective.

Danish producer prices are generally the lowest in Western Europe, although the producer price of barley is lower in the United Kingdom and Ireland than in Denmark. The prices of bacon pigs and milk are also lower in Ireland than in Denmark, and the price of wheat is lower in the United Kingdom. In none of these cases, however, except for milk in Ireland, is the price significantly less than in Denmark. The producer price of most products in most Western

TABLE 2

European Producer Prices, 1965/66-1968/69 (Average)
($ per 100 Kg.)

Country	Milk	Beef Cattle (live weight)	Bacon Pigs (dead weight, 60-75 Kg.)	Wheat	Barley
Belgium-Luxembourg	9.00	72.82	83.35	9.55	8.12
France	8.41	65.86	–	8.69	7.28
West Germany	9.57	59.52	80.33	10.20	9.26
Netherlands	9.08	66.22	74.86	9.89	8.64
Denmark	6.65	38.37	69.07	7.09	6.72
Norway	12.43	60.06	84.79	12.97	11.97
Sweden	11.19	60.12	88.01	9.57	8.85
Switzerland	12.90	85.60	–	–	8.87
Ireland	5.23	40.43	66.17	9.19	5.90
United Kingdom	9.20	50.77	72.19	6.85	6.57

Source: IFAP figures.

TABLE 3

Indices of European Producer Prices, 1965/66-1968/69
(Denmark = 100)

Country	Milk	Beef Cattle	Bacon Pigs	Wheat	Barley
Belgium-Luxembourg	135.3	190.0	120.7	134.7	120.8
France	126.5	171.6	–	122.6	108.3
West Germany	143.9	155.1	116.3	143.9	137.8
Netherlands	136.5	172.6	108.4	139.5	128.6
Denmark	100.0	100.0	100.0	100.0	100.0
Norway	186.9	156.5	122.8	182.9	178.1
Sweden	168.3	156.7	127.4	135.0	131.7
Switzerland	194.0	446.2	–	–	132.0
Ireland	78.7	105.4	95.8	129.6	87.8
United Kingdom	138.3	132.3	104.5	96.6	97.8

Source: IFAP figures.

European countries is within a range of 20-100 per cent above the
Danish price, with the striking exceptions of milk and beef cattle in
Switzerland, which are, respectively, nearly twice and more than
four times the Danish price. Also outside the 20-100 per cent range
were barley in France and bacon pigs in the Netherlands, which were
only some 8 per cent above the Danish price.

By country, the over-all picture that emerges is of Denmark
and Ireland as low-cost producers, with the exception of wheat in
Ireland; the United Kingdom as a low-cost producer, except for milk
and beef cattle; and all the other countries as high-cost producers
for all commodities, except for bacon pigs in the Netherlands and
barley in France. More detailed study of these rather fragmentary
price data, covering as large a number of countries as possible, is
needed, but the general world picture is clear enough.

If one examines Table 4 in conjunction with Tables 1-3, the
tendency for countries that are high-cost producers to expand their
exports at the expense of low-cost producers becomes obvious. Total
cereals exports (in tonnages) from Argentina rose by nearly 60 per
cent and from the United States rose by some 40 per cent between the
1959-63 period and the 1964-68 period, whereas, between the same two
periods, exports from Canada rose by about 32 per cent and those from
Australia by almost 75 per cent, but French exports of cereals rose by
approximately 130 per cent.

In meat, the largest increase in exports between the two periods
was from the Netherlands, which more than doubled its tonnages, whereas
exports from Denmark, Ireland, Argentina, and the United States rose
by only 10-50 per cent, and from Yugoslavia by 70 per cent. The most
alarming picture is shown by trends in butter exports. Tonnages
exported by Denmark, Poland, the USSR, and Australia fell (in the case
of Australia very sharply, to less than half the figure of the earlier
five-year period); exports from New Zealand rose by about 14 per
cent; and exports from France and the Netherlands rose by about 45
per cent and 22 per cent, respectively.

A similar trend is shown in exports of cheese, although here the
picture is complicated by differences in type, for cheese is a much
less uniform product than butter. This may partly account for the substantial rise in exports of cheese from West Germany and Switzerland,
the highest-cost producers of milk in the world among exporting countries
by a very large margin. Exports of cheese from Denmark and the
United States fell, and exports form Australia rose by 40 per cent and
from New Zealand by a little under 10 per cent, whereas exports

TABLE 4

Exports of Selected Agricultural Products, 1959-69

Country	1959-63 (annual average)	1964-68 (annual average)	1969	1959-63 (annual average)	1964-68 (annual average)	1969
	Exports of Cereals					
	100,000 Metric Tons			$10 Million		
France	33.6	78.3	122.9	20.0	54.7	88.9
USSR	73.4	51.2	80.3	50.2	35.1	55.5
Canada	105.8	139.3	81.2	68.5	94.2	55.9
United States	302.3	422.3	322.5	182.9	265.0	205.2
Argentina	55.3	87.5	83.8	28.6	47.3	42.6
Australia	43.0	75.1	63.2	29.3	44.5	37.3
World	747.0	1,047.6	937.3	473.8	703.2	707.5
	Exports of Meat (fresh, chilled, or frozen)					
	10,000 Metric Tons			Million $		
Denmark	18.0	23.7	19.7	11.6	17.3	15.1
France	11.3	12.7	14.8	6.5	9.7	12.1
Ireland	8.2	12.7	16.4	5.8	9.3	12.9
Netherlands	15.0	30.3	43.2	11.4	28.1	43.8
Yugoslavia	6.4	11.3	8.8	3.9	9.7	8.2
United States	16.9	20.9	23.2	9.8	13.4	17.2
Argentina	46.6	50.5	57.8	17.7	26.3	30.2
World	242.9	360.3	426.1	140.2	295.8	304.6
	Exports of Butter					
	1,000 Metric Tons			Million $		
Denmark	114.6	108.4	99.8	100.0	103.5	80.9
France	31.5	45.5	71.1	28.4	47.8	82.5
Netherlands	36.7	45.1	48.8	33.0	36.0	35.6
Poland	24.8	20.1	9.3	18.1	14.9	—
USSR	61.6	52.2	—	44.4	42.3	—
Australia	209.8	91.2	78.4	186.5	65.8	46.6
New Zealand	172.2	195.5	216.5	130.9	149.0	135.0
World	623.4	723.9	—	504.0	603.7	—

12

Country	1959-63 (annual average)	1964-68 (annual average)	1969	1959-63 (annual average)	1964-68 (annual average)	1969
	Exports of Cheese (including curd)					
	1,000 Metric Tons			Million $		
Denmark	78.9	75.9	61.9	49.0	57.0	50.6
France	36.1	74.2	90.9	34.0	73.9	106.2
West Germany	14.0	31.3	48.9	11.7	31.0	54.8
Italy	24.1	22.7	24.3	28.6	36.9	40.2
Netherlands	109.9	129.6	163.5	65.5	100.6	143.3
Switzerland	31.9	40.0	48.0	37.3	51.9	66.3
Canada	10.1	15.6	16.5	7.4	11.9	13.3
United States	6.6	3.1	3.3	5.7	4.0	4.4
Australia	20.2	28.4	34.2	11.4	16.7	18.7
New Zealand	88.1	96.7	92.5	54.4	55.2	50.8
World	503.5	649.5	—	356.1	531.0	—

Country	1959-63 (annual average)	1964-68 (annual average)	1969
	Exports of Eggs (shell, dried, liquid, and frozen)		
	Million $		
Belgium-Luxembourg	16.0	21.0	42.8
Denmark	40.1	13.0	11.8
Netherlands	103.6	53.1	56.9
Poland	27.9	17.1	--
United States	17.3	13.3	14.0
China (Mainland)	16.5 [a]	32.9	--
World	285.5	229.6	--

[a]Average of 4 years, 1960-63 inclusive.

Source: FAO, Commerce Yearbook (Rome, annual publication).

13

from France more than doubled and those from West Germany nearly trebled.

Exports of eggs have been considerably reduced by a trend toward self-sufficiency in the main importing countries—Great Britain, West Germany, and Italy—which is probably more the result of new production methods than of government policy or price supports in the importing countries, but it is significant that, of the main exporting countries, the fall in exports was sharpest for the lowest-cost producer, Denmark.

In fact, the trend toward expansion of exports by high-cost producers at the expense of low-cost producers is probably more serious than these tables indicate for two reasons. First, although harmonization of agricultural producer prices within the EEC has led to a fall in some producer prices in West Germany and Italy, the highest-cost producers of temperate-zone products, it has led to a rise in prices in France and the Netherlands, which were the lowest-cost producers within the six EEC nations. The two latter countries could at the end of the 1950's be regarded as medium-cost (or, for some products, even low-cost) producers in a world comparison but, by the early 1970's, should be regarded as high-cost producers for most temperate-zone agricultural products. Second, the trend for exports of low-cost producers to decline, relatively and in some cases absolutely, has continued and possibly accelerated in the years since 1959; in other words, the trend has been a continuing and progressive one.

Conversely, Chapter 2, below, seems to suggest that the trade diversion effect of the EEC CAP during the years 1958-69 was not entirely due to an increase in the degree of protection accorded to the EEC producers as a whole against the outside world (except possibly in poultry and pigmeat), but to the removal of most barriers to agricultural trade within the EEC. If this interpretation is correct, the trade diversion effect may diminish or end with the completion of the CAP in 1970.

Even if it does not continue, however, the shift that has taken place in the 1960's together with the high degree of agricultural protection that existed in the Common Market countries at the start of the period, is serious; while the British entry into the Common Market raises the possibility of much greater effects on nonmember countries, because of British predominance as a food-importing country.

NOTES

1. The reasons are summarized in F. Lamartine Yates, Food, Land and Manpower in Western Europe (London: Macmillan, 1960); and in E. F. Nash and E. A. Attwood, The Agricultural Policies of Britain and Denmark (London: Land Books, 1961).

2. H. Heaton, Economic History of Europe (New York: Harper & Bros., 1948), p. 435.

3. GATT, Trends in International Trade: A Report by a Panel of Experts (Geneva, 1958).

2

**THE EEC
AND AGRICULTURE**

THE DEVELOPMENT OF THE CAP

The Treaty of Rome, signed on March 25, 1957, provided that the Common Market should extend to agriculture, which is dealt with in Articles 38-47. The aims of the CAP, set out in Article 39, are as follows:

a) to increase agricultural productivity by developing technical progress, by ensuring the rational development of agricultural policy, especially labour;

b) to ensure thereby a fair standard of living for the agricultural population, particularly by the increasing of the individual earnings of persons engaged in agriculture;

c) to stabilise markets;

d) to guarantee regular supplies; and

e) to ensure reasonable prices to consumers.

Article 39 continues:

2. In the working out of the common agricultural policy and the special methods which it may involve, due account should be taken of:

a) the exceptional character of agricultural activities, arising from the social character of agriculture, and from the structural and natural disparities of the various agricultural regions;

17

b) the need to make the appropriate adjustments gradually;
and

c) the fact that in Member States, agriculture constitutes
a sector which is closely linked to the economy as a whole.

It is clear from this Article that agriculture is to be regarded
in some ways as a special case, but the Treaty of Rome provided little
practical guidance on the working out of the CAP. There is no indication of the level at which producer prices are to be set, the degree
of self-sufficiency to be aimed at, or the degree of protection against
imports from outside the EEC (all these questions are closely related,
the last two depending essentially on the first, the level of producer
prices).

The higher proportion of the working population engaged in
agriculture in the six EEC nations compared with Great Britain made
it inevitable, however, that protection for agriculture in the EEC would
be through import restriction, as done previously in the individual
countries that made up the Common Market, rather than by subsidies,
as in Great Britain. The Treaty of Rome also clearly specified free
trade in agricultural products within the EEC and a unified policy
toward third countries, but the method of agricultural support and
protection (including the levy system and the designated expenditures
as later developed) was not indicated.

Article 43 of the Treaty of Rome provided that "in order to
formulate the guiding lines of a common agricultural policy the
Commission shall, upon the date of entry into force of this Treaty,
convene a conference of Member States" and, accordingly, the Stresa
Conference met in July, 1958, under the chairmanship of Dr. Sicco
Mansholt, former Netherlands minister of agriculture and the member
of the EEC Commission responsible for agriculture. The Stresa
Conference had to analyze the existing situation (there was a lack at
the time of such basic information as the percentage of the labor force
in agriculture in some of the member states), as well as the current
policies of the governments of the six EEC nations, and to make
recommendations for a common future policy.

Draft regulations based on the work of the Stresa Conference
were then drawn up by the EEC Commission and, as provided for in
the Treaty of Rome, submitted to the Council of Ministers early in
1960. The Council reached agreement on them by June. After discussions lasting throughout 1961, when for a time it seemed that
further progress would be blocked by the divergent interests of the

six countries, agreement was reached on January 14, 1962, on the regulations that laid the foundations of the CAP. (The agreement was the first of a series of negotiating marathons and clock-stopping procedures intended to comply with the December 31, 1961, deadline for the end of the first stage of the transition period.)

The January, 1962, agreement, on regulations, which came into effect in August, 1962, concerned the gradual establishment of a common organization of markets in cereals, pigmeat, eggs, poultry, vegetables, and wine (Nos. 19-24); the financing of the CAP (No. 25); and the application of rules of competition to production and trade in agricultural products (No, 26).

The next important step was the agreement reached on December 23, 1963, on proposals for the organization of markets for beef and veal, dairy products, and rice, to come into effect late in 1964, and also for the principle for a common policy in oils and fats. The products involved in the January, 1962, and December, 1963, agreements accounted for some 95 per cent of the total value of EEC agricultural production.

The system of protection and regulation adopted for grains set the pattern for other agricultural products, since meat and dairy product prices depend largely on the price of feed grains, and all grain prices are interrelated. The system adopted was that of a variable levy on imports from nonmember countries equal to the difference between the internal producer price and the fluctuating world market price; obligatory intervention of the EEC domestic market when prices fell 5-10 per cent below the target price, which (for grains) is set each year in advance of the harvest season; and a subsidy on exports to nonmember countries equal to the difference between the internal and the world market price.

The same system of protection used for grains was adopted for beef, veal, and pigmeat, except that, with these commodities, the levy on imports from third countries consists of two elements: one to compensate for the difference between world market and internal EEC prices for feed grains, and an additional element to give protection to domestic EEC producers. In the case of pigmeat, eggs, and poultry, the latter is a 7 per cent tariff based on the sluice-gate price for the previous year; for beef and veal, there is a fixed 20 per cent customs duty and, for live cattle, a fixed 16 per cent duty, as well as a protective element (which is not pre-determined as in eggs, poultry, and pigmeat) in the variable levy.

In addition to the introduction of the permanent system of organization and support, the January, 1962, agreement provided for the gradual elimination of import restrictions between the six EEC nations and of subsidies and other distortions of competition. At the outset, there were very large differences in grain prices between West Germany, on the one hand, and the lower-cost producers in the EEC, especially France (for barley) and the Netherlands (for wheat), on the other hand. This problem was dealt with in the December, 1964, agreement, where the Council of Ministers agreed on uniform prices, to become effective on July 1, 1967, that were slightly above halfway between the high West German and the low French prices. West German farmers were to receive compensation for two years after the introduction of the common prices.

Parallel with the development of the common policy on prices and on levies on imports from third countries was the equally crucial development of the common policy on financing of the CAP. In January, 1962, the Council of Ministers agreed on the financing of the CAP during the first stage of the transition period until mid-1965. The question of financing after that year was the cause of the crisis of July, 1965, which led to a seven-month French absence from the Council of Ministers. Negotiations were resumed in May, 1966, when financing agreements to the end of the third stage of the transition period, 1969, were agreed upon. The May, 1966, agreements also advanced the date of a full customs union, with abolition of obstacles to industrial trade between the six EEC nations, by eighteen months from the original target date of January 1, 1970, to July 1, 1968. (Chapter 4 deals with this subject in greater detail.)

THE TRADE DIVERSION EFFECT OF THE CAP

Between 1959 and 1969, total EEC imports of food and live animals from all sources (including intra- EEC trade) more than doubled, rising from $4,531 million to $10,511 million. In the same period, however, food imports by the six Common Market countries from each other increased nearly fivefold, from $1,040 million to $4,471 million, whereas imports from nonmember countries rose from $3,491 million to $6,040 million. (See Table 5.)

Since these figures include tropical products—such as tea, coffee, and cocoa—that are not produced in the EEC and other products—such as oranges and bananas—that are produced only to a limited extent, and since these products figure more largely in the imports from third countries than in intra-EEC trading, the trade diversion effect was larger than appears from these figures.

TABLE 5

Source of EEC Food Imports, 1959-69

Food and Live Animals (SITC Section 0*)

Year	World	EEC	Non-EEC	EFTA	Eastern Europe	Canada	United States	Australia	New Zealand	Union of South Africa	Central & South America	Denmark	Yugoslavia	Ireland
							(Million $)							
1959	4,531	1,040	3,491	497	199	122	427	59	6	39	857	292	50	11
1960	4,860	1,192	3,668	481	223	133	438	62	18	39	973	272	62	10
1961	5,049	1,302	3,747	478	268	167	580	80	3	57	835	264	63	15
1962	5,811	1,467	4,344	524	272	143	710	78	8	91	1,054	261	70	13
1963	6,352	1,672	4,680	623	329	150	738	51	8	91	1,109	314	119	20
1964	6,988	1,921	5,067	631	295	138	820	61	14	85	1,322	303	102	48
1965	8,028	2,388	5,640	681	397	153	996	67	20	75	1,481	311	112	49
1966	8,469	2,554	5,915	642	451	162	1,126	69	17	76	1,508	288	132	34
1967	8,525	2,814	5,711	672	499	150	872	70	14	87	1,443	241	165	24
1968	9,017	3,406	5,611	597	560	128	919	56	8	127	1,382	238	113	18
1969	10,511	4,471	6,040	647	577	123	861	73	13	91	1,526	253	148	24
							Per Cent							
1959	100.0	23.0	77.0	11.0	4.4	2.7	9.4	1.3	0.1	0.9	18.9	6.4	1.1	0.2
1960	100.0	24.5	75.5	9.9	4.6	2.7	9.0	1.3	0.4	0.8	20.0	5.6	1.3	0.2
1961	100.0	25.8	74.2	9.5	5.3	3.3	11.5	1.6	-	1.1	16.5	5.2	1.2	0.2
1962	100.0	25.2	74.8	9.0	4.7	2.5	12.2	1.3	0.1	1.6	18.1	4.5	1.2	0.2
1963	100.0	26.3	73.7	9.8	5.2	2.4	11.6	0.8	0.1	1.4	17.5	4.9	1.9	0.3
1964	100.0	27.5	72.5	9.0	4.2	2.0	11.7	0.9	0.2	1.2	18.9	4.3	1.5	0.7
1965	100.0	29.7	70.3	8.5	4.9	1.9	12.4	0.8	0.2	0.9	18.4	3.9	1.4	0.6
1966	100.0	30.2	69.8	7.6	5.3	1.9	13.3	0.8	0.2	0.9	17.8	3.4	1.6	0.4
1967	100.0	33.0	67.0	7.9	5.9	1.8	10.2	0.8	0.2	1.0	16.9	2.8	1.9	0.3
1968	100.0	37.8	62.2	6.6	6.2	1.4	10.2	0.6	0.1	1.4	15.3	2.6	1.3	0.2
1969	100.0	42.5	57.5	6.2	5.5	1.2	8.2	0.7	0.9	0.9	14.5	2.4	1.4	0.2

Source: OECD, Foreign Trade Statistics, "Series B" (Parts, annual publication), percentages derived.

*Standard International Trade Classification, revised classification, Statistical Papers Series M, No. 34 (New York: United Nations, 1961).

It is clear from Table 5 that the most seriously affected of the main suppliers of all foodstuffs to the EEC has been Denmark, whose total food exports to the six EEC nations fell from $292 million in 1959 to $253 million in 1969, and Canada, whose total food exports were almost the same at the end of the period as at the beginning (after a rise in the mid-1960's). Despite the amount of attention that has been focused on U.S. exports to the EEC countries, these were nearly twice as large in 1969 as they were ten years earlier, although they were perceptibly lower in 1969 than in the four preceding years.

The value of exports from Eastern Europe to the EEC nearly trebled, even though one might expect these to have been affected by the development of the CAP nearly as much as Denmark's exports, in view of the similar character of the products. Yugoslavia's exports to the EEC countries also nearly trebled. Exports from Australia, New Zealand, and the Union of South Africa to the Common Market countries are so small that trends are not very significant, but exports from all three, particularly that last, have risen.

In the main commodity groups, the largest trade diversion effect was felt in dairy products and eggs. (See Table 6.) Imports by the six EEC nations from each other rose from $220 million in 1959 to $662 million in 1969, whereas imports from outside the EEC fell from $223 million to $110 million. Much the largest impact of this fall was felt by Denmark, whose exports of dairy products and eggs to the EEC countries fell from $99 million in 1959 to $21 million in 1969. There was also a significant development in U.S. dairy exports to the six EEC nations, which rose erratically from $10 million in 1959 to $52 million in 1964 and fell to $2 million in 1969. Exports from Eastern Europe showed a similar trend, rising from $25 million in 1959 to $38 million both in 1962 and 1963 and falling to $10 million in 1969.

This bulge of EEC imports in the mid-1960's with a fall after 1965 or 1966, also appears, for example, in U.S. exports to the EEC of fruit and vegetables and meat, and U.S. and Canadian imports of cereals. The likely explanation is the effect of higher incomes in the EEC making themselves felt on imports from third countries until 1964-65, with a fall in later years as the CAP was completed and tightened. If so, it would be reasonable to suppose that, in the absence of the CAP, imports from third countries would have continued to rise.

The simplest way of illustrating the trade diversion effect of the CAP is to compare figures of the degree of self-sufficiency at the start and end of the coming into force of the CAP with figures of the

TABLE 6

Source of EEC Food Imports, by Commodity Groups, 1959–69
(Million $)

Year	World	EEC	Non-EEC	EFTA	Eastern Europe	Canada	United States	Central & South America	Den-mark	Yugo-slavia	Ire-land
Live Animals (SITC Division 00)											
1959	215	38	177	116	40	n.a.	n.a.	n.a.	79	11	3
1960	274	70	204	115	54	n.a.	n.a.	n.a.	78	12	5
1961	263	55	208	128	44	n.a.	1	n.a.	85	17	8
1962	240	49	191	110	48	n.a.	2	n.a.	68	22	4
1963	327	92	235	131	57	1	2	1	72	31	6
1964	384	108	276	149	69	1	2	6	71	18	22
1965	448	114	334	179	100	2	4	6	80	13	22
1966	401	97	304	106	144	3	5	4	54	22	13
1967	443	164	279	95	135	2	4	1	35	33	6
1968	507	235	272	89	141	1	3	n.a.	44	31	4
1969	708	325	383	122	205	2	4	1	58	42	2
Meat and Meat Preparations (SITC Division 01)											
1959	368	117	251	90	31	3	34	75	69	11	5
1960	439	119	320	84	35	1	42	59	83	16	2
1961	382	150	232	128	32	1	56	61	74	13	3
1962	464	181	283	110	35	1	71	69	66	22	4
1963	665	260	405	136	56	1	48	94	63	48	9
1964	895	321	574	134	66	2	74	190	53	53	24
1965	1,002	400	602	125	87	3	71	177	53	65	23
1966	1,065	422	643	147	121	3	68	183	51	64	16
1967	1,120	489	631	150	134	3	55	170	36	75	9
1968	1,181	678	503	118	123	3	45	126	86	53	11
1969	1,249	800	449	145	146	2	52	178	77	49	15

(Continued)

23

Table 6 (Continued)

Year	World	EEC	Non-EEC	EFTA	Eastern Europe	Canada	United States	Central & South America	Denmark	Yugoslavia	Ireland
					Dairy Products and Eggs (SITC Division 02)						
1959	443	220	223	132	25	5	10	14	99	n.a.	n.a.
1960	443	230	213	104	34	2	8	14	75	n.a.	n.a.
1961	414	221	193	108	42	1	5	6	74	n.a.	n.a.
1962	425	232	193	106	38	1	5	5	71	4	2
1963	456	253	203	106	38	1	18	4	116	4	2
1964	446	252	194	89	18	8	52	1	53	3	n.a.
1965	531	331	200	98	22	10	38	5	53	3	n.a.
1966	557	378	179	103	22	4	13	n.a.	1	3	1
1967	578	420	158	102	24	4	2	1	36	2	2
1968	647	529	118	92	14	2	1	n.a.	27	2	2
1969	772	662	110	87	10	2	2	n.a.	21	n.a.	2
					Fish and Fish Preparations (SITC Division 03)						
1959	180	39	141	68	3	1	1	n.a.	20	3	2
1960	207	43	164	72	3	4	2	n.a.	20	4	2
1961	240	53	187	81	8	4	2	1	25	5	n.a.
1962	273	59	214	97	8	6	2	1	33	5	2
1963	308	62	246	101	10	10	4	5	35	5	2
1964	328	69	259	112	12	12	5	7	42	5	2
1965	381	82	299	130	22	10	9	7	47	4	2
1966	387	96	301	122	14	13	10	8	47	3	3
1967	406	103	303	120	14	14	11	8	47	4	3
1968	448	117	331	124	20	15	9	7	55	4	3
1969	474	133	341	130	21	17	13	7	58	4	4

| | | | | | | | | Central & | | | |
Year	World	EEC	Non-EEC	EFTA	Eastern Europe	Canada	United States	South America	Den-mark	Yugo-slavia	Ire-land
Cereals and Cereal Preparations (SITC Division 04)											
1959	933	98	835	39	54	109	292	140	13	9	n.a.
1960	985	127	858	42	53	123	282	215	7	14	n.a.
1961	1,143	178	965	45	87	160	402	132	5	7	n.a.
1962	1,329	158	1,171	66	67	132	450	256	10	1	1
1963	1,244	202	1,042	47	62	133	446	216	12	4	n.a.
1964	1,306	283	1,023	38	44	113	468	265	9	1	n.a.
1965	1,618	387	1,231	57	49	122	602	340	18	3	n.a.
1966	1,748	403	1,345	63	18	135	715	329	12	6	n.a.
1967	1,596	426	1,170	79	61	121	483	304	10	29	n.a.
1968	1,682	534	1,148	62	41	104	551	268	3	14	n.a.
1969	1,806	828	978	38	52	94	437	267	12	8	n.a.
Fruit and Vegetables (SITC Division 05)											
1959	1,138	398	740	25	24	n.a.	54	90	7	11	n.a.
1960	1,234	416	818	17	28	1	62	145	5	8	n.a.
1961	1,367	482	885	21	39	1	72	149	5	12	n.a.
1962	1,645	603	1,042	24	50	3	94	156	4	16	n.a.
1963	1,666	570	1,096	26	51	3	103	166	7	16	n.a.
1964	1,725	615	1,110	22	52	3	90	153	6	17	n.a.
1965	2,136	779	1,357	24	93	4	108	239	3	17	n.a.
1966	2,199	801	1,398	27	98	4	94	251	3	15	n.a.
1967	2,239	833	1,406	29	91	4	89	267	3	18	n.a.
1968	2,221	853	1,368	30	93	3	65	307	3	13	n.a.
1969	2,623	1,075	1,548	42	114	5	65	324	4	25	n.a.

(Continued)

Table 6 (Continued)

Animal Foodstuffs (excluding unmilled cereals) (SITC Division 08)

Year	World	EEC	Non-EEC	EFTA	Eastern Europe	Canada	United States	Central & South America	Denmark	Yugoslavia	Ireland
1959	284	61	223	22	8	1	26	92	6	1	n.a.
1960	279	60	219	14	8	1	31	98	2	1	n.a.
1961	286	70	216	14	10	1	24	109	3	n.a.	n.a.
1962	438	73	365	17	14	n.a.	73	169	6	n.a.	n.a.
1963	491	85	406	21	7	n.a.	97	176	5	2	n.a.
1964	541	112	429	27	2	n.a.	110	180	7	1	n.a.
1965	643	110	533	40	4	1	153	208	11	2	n.a.
1966	787	138	649	45	15	1	210	244	11	3	n.a.
1967	779	141	638	54	19	n.a.	219	213	16	1	n.a.
1968	824	166	658	52	19	n.a.	215	218	17	4	n.a.
1969	947	218	729	51	18	1	260	263	20	3	n.a.

Source: OECD, Foreign Trade Statistics, "Series B" (Paris, annual publication).

percentage of EEC imports that came from EEC and non-EEC sources
in the same years. The latter figures—the percentage of imports from
EEC and non-EEC sources—underestimate the trade diversion effect
if there has been an increase in national self-sufficiency in each country
within the Common Market or in the main importing country within
the six EEC nations. This would result in a decline in the share of
imports in total <u>consumption.</u> The reverse would happen if national
self-sufficiency fell. The import figures also do not show the extent
to which the EEC may have become a lower net importer, or larger
net exporter, of certain products during the period of the development.
of the CAP.

Direct comparisons between the start of the CAP and 1969 can
not be made with the available figures of self-sufficiency for several
commodities because the figures for 1958 and 1965 cited in Table 7,
from the Mansholt Committee's Report of 1968, are in different categories from the later EEC tables from which the figures for 1967-68,
1968-69, and 1969-70 are taken.

Comparisons covering the whole period are possible, however,
for "all grains," sugar, pigmeat, and poultry. The degree of self-
sufficiency of the six EEC nations for all grains rose perceptibly,
from 85 at the start of the period to 91 in 1969-70. (It was 94 in
1968-69). The degree of self-sufficiency for pigmeat remained the
same at about 99-100, whereas the degree of self-sufficiency for
poultry rose from 93 to 98 and for sugar from 99 to 110.

As in other importing countries, such as Great Britain, some
in self-sufficiency might perhaps have been expected in some products
as the result of technical progress, but, if this were the main cause,
one would expect imports from EEC and non-EEC sources to be affected equally. The figures in Table 7 show that this has not happened.

In all the groups of temperate-zone foodstuffs except fruit and
vegetables, fish and fish preparations, and animal foodstuffs there
has been a considerable trade diversion effect. (Animal foodstuffs
probably should not be classified under temperate-zone foodstuffs, as
it is a heterogenous collection, including animal and vegetable oils,
and its, in any case, the smallest of the groups in EEC imports; it is
nonetheless included here for completeness.)

As noted earlier in this chapter, much the largest trade diversion
effect has been in dairy products and eggs. The other three main
groups of temperate-zone products—live animals, meat, and cereals—
have also been considerably affected. Imports of cereals and cereal

TABLE 7

Degree of EEC Self-Sufficiency, 1958-1969/70

Product	1958	1965	1967-68	1968-69	1969-70
Hard wheat	–	–	77	60	75
Soft wheat	93	104	118	120	105
Barley	–	–	95	107	104
Feed grains	78	73	–	–	–
All grains	85	85	91	94	91
Sugar	99	100	95	103	110
Beef	89	85			
Veal	102	93	89	89	–
Pigmeat	100	99	100	99	–
Poultry	93	96	98	98	–
Milk and milk products	103	103	–	–	–
Butter	–	–	117	113	–
Cheese	–	–	103	102	–

Sources: Figures for 1958 and 1965 from EEC Commission, Memorandum on the Reform of Agriculture in the European Economic Community, "COM (68) 1,000" (Brussels, 1968), Annex, Table 14A; figures for 1967-68, 1968-69, and 1969-70 from EEC Commission, Yearbook of Agricultural Statistics, 1970 (Brussels, 1971).

28

TABLE 8

Percentage of EEC Food Imports from
Non-EEC Sources, 1959 and 1969

Product	1959	1969
Live animals	82	54
Meat and meat preparations	68	35
Dairy products and eggs	53	14
Fish and fish preparations	78	72
Cereals and cereal preparations	90	54
Fruit and vegetables	65	59
Animal foodstuffs (excluding unmilled cereals)	78	76
Temperate-zone foodstuffs (all the above)	71	53
All foodstuffs (the above plus coffee, tea, cocoa, and sugar)	77	57

Source: Figures derived from Table 6, above.

preparations by members of the six EEC nations from each other rose
ninefold, whereas imports from nonmember countries were only some
16 per cent higher in 1969 than in 1959. Imports of cereals from
Canada, the European Free Trade Association (EFTA) countries, and
Eastern Europe fell or remained about the same, whereas imports
from the United States rose by about 50 per cent and those from Central
and South America nearly doubled.

Imports of meat and meat preparations from EEC countries rose
sevenfold, whereas imports from non-EEC sources rose only by about
70 per cent. Again, the main adverse impact was on Denmark, whereas
imports from Eastern Europe, Yugoslavia, the United States, and
Central and South America rose significantly. Imports of live animals
from EEC countries increased ninefold, whereas imports from non-
EEC countries more than doubled. In this case also, the only important

supplier whose exports to the EEC actually fell significantly was Denmark. It is rather mysterious why exports of meat and live animals from Eastern Europe and Yugoslavia have risen, while those from Denmark have either fallen or risen only slightly; the fact that East Germany is not subject to EEC agricultural levies may be relevant here.

As mentioned earlier, fruit and vegetables and animal foodstuffs have not been much affected by the CAP, the percentage of imports from non-EEC sources being only about 2-6 per cent lower in 1969 than in 1959. As might be expected, since a common policy for fish was not put into operation until February 1971, fish and fish products have also been only slightly affected.

The import figures in Tables 6 and 8 reflect monetary measurements. There has not been a very large divergence of the trend of world market and EEC prices during the period under consideration, except in meat, so that, if imports were expressed in quantities, the result would not be very different. With regard to meat, the prices of EEC beef and veal have risen less than, and poultry and pigmeat more than, world market prices. (See Table 17.) Since the two latter products are a larger part of total EEC imports than beef and veal are, the figures in Tables 6 and 8 may understate the extent of the trade diversion effect in meat, compared with the results that would be obtained from examining tonnage figures.

Except in dairy products, where the impact on outside suppliers—particularly Denmark—has been almost catastrophic, and also in Danish exports of meat and live animals, the CAP has not led to a severe fall in the value of food imports from third countries for any of the main commodity groups or for any of the main third-country suppliers—Eastern Europe, Yugoslavia, Canada, the United States, and Central and South America.

But, despite this, the trade diversion effect of the CAP has been substantial, as shown by the fall in the percentage of all EEC imports of temperate-zone foodstuffs from non-EEC countries from 71 in 1959 to 53 in 1969. A glance at Table 6 shows that this has been a steady trend and is not the result of arbitrarily selected base or terminal years.

These figures, from the Organization for Economic Cooperation and Development, (OECD) Foreign Trade Statistics, show the effect of the CAP on broad commodity groups. More detailed data can be found for commodities and countries for those products where the impact of the CAP has been most serious—namely, meat and dairy products—in Tables 9-15.

TABLE 9

EEC Imports of Live Cattle, 1961-70

(Thousands)

Country	1961	1962	1963	1964	1965	1966	1967	1968	1969	1970
Belgium-Luxembourg	7	11	80	25	19	54	102	126	127	91
France	77	70	153	127	162	133	187	401	506	694
West Germany	—	—	47	92	122	112	303	427	544	588
Italy	—	1	—	—	—	—	—	—	—	—
Netherlands	133	63	69	40	62	31	76	58	62	66
Total EEC	217	133	349	284	365	330	668	1,012	1,239	1,439
United Kingdom	27	19	23	157	218	90	91	18	42	57
Ireland	33	14	21	77	80	49	28	10	3	10
Austria	85	106	146	78	94	79	150	175	159	114
Denmark	354	290	328	238	253	151	92	143	164	107
Yugoslavia	48	52	89	40	22	47	73	110	101	61
Hungary	70	82	131	92	123	155	170	192	235	207
Poland	7	38	45	68	90	146	113	124	198	241
Total Non-EEC	876	754	1,189	836	1,002	1,003	1,019	1,119	1,351	1,124
EEC exports	273	773	404	34	41	26	16	13	13	15
Net EEC imports	603	581	785	802	961	977	1,003	1,106	1,338	1,109

Source: CEC, "Meat" (London: annual publication).

TABLE 10

EEC Imports of Beef and Veal, 1961–70
(Thousand Tons)

Country	1961	1962	1963	1964	1965	1966	1967	1968	1969	1970
Belgium–Luxembourg	1	2	9	2	2	7	12	14	12	14
France	58	61	58	54	58	68	80	126	110	77
West Germany	3	5	4	4	2	4	14	26	37	42
Italy	–	–	–	–	–	–	–	–	–	–
Netherlands	17	29	49	62	64	54	59	73	87	105
Total EEC	79	96	120	122	126	134	166	240	246	238
United Kingdom	–	–	1	5	7	4	7	–	5	6
Ireland	4	2	5	13	18	7	1	–	–	1
Austria	–	3	2	–	–	4	–	–	–	–
Denmark	9	29	65	51	49	62	63	63	56	50
Yugoslavia	3	9	37	36	43	39	53	38	27	23
Argentina	66	86	128	192	127	123	147	82	119	108
Total non-EEC	180	244	277	399	369	345	390	294	351	363
EEC exports	137	202	59	21	16	22	28	53	28	30
Net EEC imports	43	42	218	378	353	323	362	241	323	333

Source: CEC, "Meat" (London: annual publication).

TABLE 11

EEC Imports of Live Pigs, 1961–70
(Thousands)

Country	1961	1962	1963	1964	1965	1966	1967	1968	1969	1970
Belgium-Luxembourg	124	77	69	141	233	153	496	717	783	1,104
France	44	96	73	3	31	12	40	3	6	100
West Germany	—	—	2	1	—	2	55	30	312	337
Italy	12	—	4	19	—	—	—	—	—	—
Netherlands	37	8	95	295	189	80	110	247	359	349
Total EEC	216	180	243	459	452	246	701	998	1,461	1,890
Denmark	179	138	127	121	191	180	141	157	167	152
Total non-EEC	810	577	470	222	395	405	224	228	325	213
EEC exports	219	223	250	5	76	13	6	8	2	2
Net EEC imports	591	354	220	217	319	392	218	220	323	211

Source: CEC, "Meat" (London: annual publication).

TABLE 12

EEC Imports of Pigmeat, 1961–70
(Thousand Tons)

Country	1961	1962	1963	1964	1965	1966	1967	1968	1969	1970
Belgium-Luxembourg	18	24	17	9	13	22	40	51	66	117
France	12	12	12	8	12	14	10	6	4	6
West Germany	1	—	2	2	1	1	1	6	15	4
Italy	1	1	1	5	5	8	3	1	3	8
Netherlands	35	27	57	74	95	84	84	123	138	199
Total EEC	67	64	89	98	127	128	138	188	226	334
Denmark	14	6	28	19	29	23	16	21	10	11
Total non-EEC	98	87	169	77	71	124	115	77	123	77
EEC exports	100	105	119	69	34	11	27	17	25	37
Net EEC imports	2a	18a	50	68	37	113	88	60	98	40

aNet EEC exports.

Source: CEC, "Meat" (London: annual publication).

34

TABLE 13

West German Cheese Imports, 1960/61-1970[a]
(Thousand Tons)

Country	1960/61	1961/62	1962/63	1963/64	1964/65	1965/66	1966/67	1967/68	1969	1970
Belgium-Luxembourg	0.6	2.9	2.9	3.3	3.9	4.9	4.3	2.9	1.3	1.1
France	3.5	6.2	11.5	18.0	23.3	21.3	23.2	24.6	25.5	30.0
Italy	0.7	0.9	1.0	0.9	1.0	1.0	1.1	1.3	1.7	2.0
Netherlands	53.0	51.3	52.1	53.3	46.5	56.7	58.9	54.2	68.8	77.4
Total EEC	57.8	61.3	67.5	75.5	74.7	83.9	87.5	83.0	97.3	110.5
Denmark	36.0	39.0	38.7	39.5	39.0	36.0	35.8	30.3	18.4	16.6
Total Non-EEC	48.6	50.4	53.9	55.6	51.8	50.8	52.3	40.6	27.5	32.4

[a] All years are crop years, with the exception of 1969 and 1970, which are calendar years.

Source: CEC, "Dairy Produce" (London: annual publication).

TABLE 14

West German Egg Imports, 1961–70
(Million Dozen)

Country	1961	1962	1963	1964	1965	1966	1967	1968	1969	1970
Belgium–Luxembourg	19.4	14.6	22.8	32.8	22.9	22.7	28.8	39.6	54.9	73.1
Netherlands	226.4	204.2	153.7	127.0	78.4	77.8	56.0	69.8	77.6	90.9
France	–	–	2.2	5.8	4.2	1.9	1.9	2.7	2.3	2.9
Denmark	73.1	54.7	39.8	8.0	6.0	5.5	2.3	3.1	2.5	0.3
Poland	29.7	23.2	7.7	0.7	1.2	2.2	0.9	0.3	0.3	–

Source: CEC, "Dairy Produce" (London: annual publication) and "Meat and Dairy Produce Bulletin" (London: monthly publication).

36

TABLE 15

West German Poultry Imports, 1961–70
(Thousand Tons)

Country	1961	1962	1963	1964	1965	1966	1967	1968	1969	1970
Belgium–Luxembourg	2.9	4.7	8.2	11.7	18.2	22.3	25.2	20.9	19.5	21.8
France	1.4	8.1	11.5	15.3	14.0	9.2	7.2	9.6	7.0	6.5
Italy	—	0.5	0.1	0.2	1.3	2.3	1.5	2.0	2.2	2.2
Netherlands	53.5	58.8	59.4	63.9	95.9	102.2	117.3	141.0	150.5	167.0
Total EEC	57.8	72.1	79.2	91.1	129.4	136.0	151.2	173.5	179.2	197.5
Denmark	40.1	37.9	36.8	27.1	11.9	8.7	2.9	2.2	2.4	2.5
United States	62.5	77.7	34.7	41.4	36.5	28.1	20.4	12.4	10.3	10.0
Poland	10.7	9.4	8.8	12.1	12.8	11.7	9.9	11.1	11.4	11.0
Total Non-EEC	123.5	97.2	100.2	90.8	71.0	58.7	43.0	37.9	35.4	37.5

Source: CEC, "Meat," (London: annual publication) and "Meat and Dairy Produce Bulletin" (London: monthly publication).

As a result of the shortage of beef and veal within the EEC, import levies were suspended in 1965, 1966, and 1967. There has been an increase in imports both of live cattle and of beef and veal from third countries, but the increases has been small in relation to that in intra-EEC trade. Intra-EEC trade in live cattle increased almost seven times between 1961 and 1970 and that in cattle meat increased threefold in the same period, whereas imports of live cattle from non-members rose by 28 per cent and that of cattle meat by about 100 per cent.

None of the individual exporters of beef and veal (mainly Argentina, Yugoslavia, and Denmark), however, has suffered a fall in exports to the EEC; but, in live cattle, although there has been an increase in total EEC imports from nonmembers, imports from Denmark and Ireland fell sharply, whereas imports from Yugoslavia, Hungary, and Poland rose. (See Tables 9 and 10.)

Total EEC imports from third countries of live pigs and pigmeat have fallen very sharply, the 1970 figure of the former being about a quarter of the 1961 figure and of the latter about 80 per cent of the 1961 figure. Imports of pigs and pigmeat from third countries were never very large; the main exporter and the main sufferer from the CAP was Denmark. (See Tables 11 and 12.)

EEC butter imports from third countries are negligible. Of the remaining temperate-zone products, apart from cereals and fruit and vegetables, the most important are eggs, poultry, and cheese, imported by West Germany, which is by far the largest importer within the six EEC nations. (Italy also imports these products.) Imports of cheese from outside the EEC (again mainly from Denmark) have fallen somewhat, whereas imports from other EEC countries have nearly doubled. (See Table 13.) West Germany imports of eggs from outside the EEC, mainly from Denmark and Poland at the start of the period, have dwindled to almost nothing. (See Table 14.) Imports of poultry by West Germany (mainly from Denmark, Poland, and the United States) have fallen substantially, whereas West Germany imports from other EEC countries have almost quadrupled. (See Table 15.)

CHANGES IN THE EEC DEGREE OF PROTECTION

This chapter has so far been examining the effect of the CAP on EEC food imports from third countries. An alternative approach would be to look at changes in the degree of protection, which is the difference between internal producer prices and world market (or import) prices. This subject will also be treated in Chapter 6, where the argument is made that the same figure can be used as a measure of agricultural efficiency.

In 1960, the U.N. Economic Commission for Europe (ECE) published the results of a study of agricultural protective margins in Western Europe from 1956-57 to 1958-59 in Economic Survey of Europe for 1960. (See Table 28.) The EEC Commission has published figures of the difference between world market prices and internal producer prices (in this case, threshold prices) for the EEC countries only. Since threshold prices are minimum import prices and since indicative and intervention prices will be higher, the degree of protection may be underestimated for the second and the third years in the comparison, but probably not by more than 5 or 10 per cent.

Table 16 provides figures for 1956-57-1958-59, derived from the U.N. ECE study, that may be compared with figures for 1967-68 and 1968-69, calculated by the EEC Commission. The basis of these figures must be examined more carefully before definitive conclusions can be drawn (in particular, any method of averaging the protective margins of the six EEC nations during the earlier period is open to question), but at first sight it appears that there has been a considerable increase in the degree of protection in all the commodities for which figures are available, with the possible exception of eggs, for which the degree of protection was about the same in 1967-68 as in the late 1950's (although it was higher in 1968-69).

TREND OF EEC AND WORLD MARKET PRICES

A comparison of the trend of EEC producer prices and world market prices should give much the same result as figures of changes in protective margins, although this method has the disadvantages of only indicating the change over a base date and of not showing the absolute level of protection, which is more important than its change is. It should be stressed also that both the margin-of-protection figures and price indexes showing the changing relationship of EEC and world market prices are subject to more serious difficulties of comparability and classification that are the trade diversion figures presented in Tables 5, 6, and 8, as well as in Tables 9-15.

Table 17 shows changes in EEC and world market prices from a base year of 1958. The trend of producer prices in the United Kingdom and the United States is also included for comparison. There does not appear to be much difference in the trend of EEC and world market wheat prices between 1958 and 1969; both have risen slightly. Conversely, wheat producer prices in the United Kingdom (inclusive of

TABLE 16

EEC Producer Prices as Per Cent of
World Market Prices, 1956/57-1968/69

Product	1956-57-1958-59	1967-68	1968-69
Wheat, soft	} 149	185	195
Wheat, hard		200	214
Barley	134	160	197
Sugar	131	438	456
Beef and veal	147	175	169
Pigmeat	118	147	153
Eggs	130	132	141
Butter	—	397	504

Sources: E. F. Nash, "Agriculture and the Common Market,"
Journal of Agricultural Economics, XV, I (May, 1962): EEC Commission, Yearbook of Agricultural Statistics, 1970 (Brussels, 1971),
p. 134.

subsidies) have fallen slightly during this period and, in the United
States, have fallen substantially. EEC and world market prices of
barley also do not appear to have diverged, although U.K producer
prices have fallen.

EEC producer prices of beef and veal have risen much less than
have world market prices, but more than U.K. or U.S. producer prices.
In pigmeat and poultry, EEC producer prices have risen much more
than have prices on the world market or in the United Kingdom and
the United States (U.S. prices for poultry have fallen considerably
since 1958). Milk and milk products raise the most serious classification difficulties, but it is not possible to observe any significant
differences between EEC, world market, and U.S. prices, although
U.K. producer prices have risen less than these.

Disregarding the position at the start of the period, it would
appear from these figures that there has been no substantial change

TABLE 17

Indices of Producer Prices, 1958-69
(1958 = 100)

Product	1963	1967	1968	1969
Wheat				
EEC	110	110	107	104
World market	103	106	101	101
United Kingdom	96	89	93	98
United States	106	94	80	72
Barley				
EEC	108	109	109	108
World market	110	111	101	108
United Kingdom	94	86	86	87
United States	100	117	112	100
Beef and veal				
EEC	116	135	140	149
World market	112	154	158	169
United Kingdom	107	117	122	131
United States	91	101	102	107
Pigmeat				
EEC	119	115	111	127
World market	101	115	92	111
United Kingdom				
Bacon (factory)	97	104	106	105
Other	110	120	112	116
United States	76	116	97	95
Poultry				
EEC	101	104	103	106
World market	86	83	92	89
United Kingdom	78	74	71	71
United States				
(1)[a]	71	68	55	58
(2)[b]	78	83	71	78
Milk and milk products				
EEC	120	134	131	131
World market				
Butter	130	126	143	130
Cheese	111	137	138	145
United Kingdom, milk	98	107	107	108
United States				
(1)[c]	101	119	125	131
(2)[d]	99	117	121	127

[a]Chickens
[b]Broilers
[c]Combined sales of milk, cream, and farm butter (all in terms of milk), average producer price.
[d]Whole milk delivered to plant and dealers, average producer price.

Sources: EEC prices: from EEC Commission, Yearbook of Agricultural Statistics, 1970 (Brussels, 1971), pp. 135-37; world market prices from FAO, "World: Average Export Unit Values of Selected Agricultural, Fishing and Forest Products," in The State of Food and Agriculture, 1970 (Rome, 1971), Annex Table IC; U.K. prices from Annual Abstract of Statistics, Central Statistical Office (London: HMSO, 1970) and U.S. prices from FAO, Production Yearbook, 1969 (Rome, 1970).

TABLE 18

World Average Unit Export Values, 1956–59
($ Per Metric Ton)

Product	1956	1957	1958	1959
Wheat	62.8	63.5	62.6	62.2
Barley	55.1	50.9	51.3	52.6
Beef and veal	418.4	437.8	503.8	577.9
Pigmeat	722.7	679.2	707.1	667.5
Cheese	742.3	709.3	636.7	741.1
Butter	927.0	784.5	641.1	897.4
Sugar (raw)	95.4	116.5	99.8	94.5

Source: FAO, The State of Food and Agriculture, 1970 (Rome, 1971).

since 1958 in the degree of protection, as indicated by divergences between EEC and world market prices, of the main cereals products and milk products, whereas the degree of protection accorded to beef and veal producers has fallen and that to pigmeat and poultry producers has risen.

There is a major difficulty in all index numbers, however, especially those based on a single year—namely, the question of whether the base year is in some sense representative. The year 1958 has been used here as the base because it was the year immediately before the establishment of the CAP. In fact, prices of some of the main food products on the world market, including wheat, barley, butter, and cheese, were depressed in 1958 compared with the preceding and/or the following years. Since, even before the start of the CAP, producer prices in the six EEC nations were effectively insulated from the world market, index numbers based on 1958 show EEC prices as having risen less, and world markets price as having risen more, that would a comparison using other years, or several years, as a base date. Table 18 illustrates the point.

Probably the only conclusion that can safely be drawn from the figures of changes in the degree of protection (Table 16) and the relative trend of EEC and world market prices (Table 17) is that the former indicates a much larger rise than the latter does in the general degree of agricultural protection in the EEC; but both these sets of figures are subject to many doubts.

3

AGRICULTURE
AND EFTA

The European Free Trade Association—Great Britain, Denmark, Norway, Sweden, Austria, Switzerland, and Portugal—was set up under the Stockholm Convention of November, 1959, following the breakdown in the 1958 negotiations for a wider European Free Trade Area embracing both the six EEC nations and the seven EFTA countries.* Although it was widely regarded as a temporary and second-best arrangement, until such time as Great Britain and the other EFTA members joined the Common Market, and despite its more limited objectives (mainly that there was no intention of moving toward political unity), EFTA has been a considerable success.

An initial 20 per cent cut in tariffs on industrial goods was made in July, 1960, and tariffs on these goods were completely abolished on December 31, 1966 (except for imports into Portugal, which end in 1980), two years ahead of schedule and one year before the abolition of industrial tariffs within the Common Market.

EFTA is a free trade association, not a customs union, and hence has no common tariff on imports from outside the association, but the "rules of origin" problem that arises in a free trade area (and that was the ostensible reason for the breakdown of the 1958 negotiations) has proved in practice to be overcome fairly easily.

Although the EFTA countries comprise only some 3 per cent of world population, they have an exceptionally high ratio of foreign

---

*Finland became an associate member of EFTA in 1961, and Iceland became a full member in 1970.

trade to gross national product (GNP) and account for about 15 per cent of total world imports. Except for Great Britain, their rate of economic growth has equaled that of the Common Market countries, and, except for Portugal and possibly Great Britain, their living standards are as high as, or higher than, those of the Common Market countries.*

Recently, EFTA has made more progress than the EEC has in the removal of one of the main nontariff barriers to trade, by harmonizing compulsory standards and labeling, and it has done so with wider organizations, such as the International Standardization Organization. EFTA suffers from two major defects, however. One is the close link of some of the countries, particularly Denmark, with the U.K. economy, such that the low rate of economic growth in the United Kingdom since the mid-1960's has seriously affected their own growth rate. (Great Britain absorbs 20 per cent of all Denmark's exports.)

The second main problem with EFTA, which is linked with the industrial predominance of Great Britain, is that the industrial exporting countries of EFTA have probably gained much more from the arrangement than have those countries whose exports include a substantial amount of agricultural and fisheries products. The latter are mainly Denmark and Portugal, but the position of Portugal has been made easier than might appear from a statistical comparison, because it is treated as an underdeveloped country for the purpose of industrial tariff cuts and (like the underdeveloped countries associated with the EEC) has been allowed free access to the markets of the other EFTA countries without having to make reciprocal tariff cuts. Also, its main nonindustrial exports—canned fish (especially sardines), cork, olives, and wine—are not in direct competition with the domestic agriculture of the other EFTA countries and so have, in some cases, been treated as industrial products.

The Stockholm Convention includes two Annexes, D and E, which cover, respectively, the agricultural and fisheries products that are excluded from the agreement and on which member states are not obliged to reduce tariffs. Table 19 shows the importance of each of these types of goods in the exports of the member countries and so

---

*GNP figures (per head) now show Great Britain to be below several of the EEC countries, but such comparisons are affected by the British currency devaluation of 1967 and may show Great Britain in an excessively poor light.

TABLE 19

EFTA Exports, 1968

Country	Total Exports (million $)	Annex D Exports (million $)	Annex E Exports (million $)	Annex D and E Exports as Percentage of Total
Austria	1,988.6	82.2	0.4	4.4
Denmark	2,582.3	914.5	73.6	38.3
Finland	1,635.7	50.1	—	3.1
Norway	1,937.5	28.5	70.6	5.1
Portugal	732.2	59.5	7.4	9.1
Sweden	4,937.3	112.3	20.1	2.8
Switzerland	4,021.4	123.2	0.4	3.7
U.K.	15,346.3	273.1	16.4	1.9

Source: EFTA Trade, 1968 (Geneva: EFTA, February, 1970), Table 16.

illustrates the probable benefit that the member countries have derived from the existence of the EFTA agreement.

The effect on total exports by EFTA countries to other EFTA members is indicated by the figures in Table 20. Great Britain's low rate of export growth merely reflects the low rate of growth of total British exports. The low rate of growth of Danish exports, however, is probably a reflection of the large proportion of its exports included in Annexes D and E of the Stockholm Convention.

Agriculture is dealt with in Articles 21-25 of the Stockholm Convention. The most important articles are 22 and 25, which read as follows:

22.1. In regard to agriculture, Member States recognise that the policies pursued by them are designed
(a) to increase productivity and the rational development of production,
(b) to promote a reasonable degree of price stability and adequate supplies to consumers at reasonable prices, and
(c) to ensure an adequate standard of living to persons engaged in agriculture.
In pursuing these policies, Member States shall have due regard to the interests of other Member States in the export of agricultural goods and shall take into consideration traditional channels of trade.

2. Having regard to these policies, the objectives of the Association shall be to facilitate an expansion of trade which will provide reasonable reciprocity to Member States whose economies depend to a great extent on exports of agricultural goods.

25. The Council shall keep the provisions of Articles 21 to 25 under review and it shall once a year consider the development of trade in agricultural goods within the area of the Association. The Council shall consider what further action shall be taken in pursuit of the objective set out in Article 22.

The method chosen of providing reasonable reciprocity to member states whose economies depend to a great extent on exports of agricultural goods was that of bilateral agreements between the countries comprising EFTA. These agreements were provided for in

TABLE 20

Increase in Total Exports to EFTA, 1959-68
(Per Cent)

Country	Increase
Austria	303.3
Denmark	128.6
Finland	156.5
Norway	163.1
Portugal	382.0
Sweden	162.9
Switzerland	204.3
U.K.	89.4
All EFTA countries	145.1

Source: EFTA Trade, 1968 (Geneva: EFTA, February, 1970), Table 80.

Article 23 of the Stockholm Convention, which states that two member states making an agreement on agricultural trade shall inform the other members and that such agreements shall remain in force as long as the treaty itself.

DANISH FARM EXPORTS TO THE
UNITED KINGDOM

It is clear from Table 19 that the problem of the agricultural member states is overwhelmingly that of Denmark. Iceland, since its accession in 1970, has encountered a similar problem regarding exports of fish. (Fish and fish products make up about 40 per cent of the value of Iceland's exports.) The food exports of Austria, Sweden, and Switzerland, although not negligible, are much smaller in relation to their total exports. Norway's fish exports have also presented a problem (particularly the dispute with Great Britain in 1969 over imports of fish fillets) but again are much smaller in relation to Norway's total exports.

A number of tariffs on British imports of food from Denmark were, in fact, removed as part of the Anglo-Danish agreement of July, 1959, but, as tariffs are much less important than other forms of import control and internal price supports are in limiting international trade in agricultural products, the benefit that Denmark derived from these concessions was not large. The 10 per cent duty that Great Britain formerly charged on Danish bacon imports was halved in July, 1960, and removed altogether a year later. The duty on tinned pork, ranging from 5 per cent to 10 per cent, was removed in the same two stages, and the 10 per cent duty on blue-veined cheese and tinned cream was abolished in July, 1960.

Also as part of the EFTA negotiations, Sweden made some concessions on agricultural imports from Denmark. The tariffs on the products concerned—meat, tinned meat, sausages, potatoes, tinned milk, butter, eggs, and egg products—remained unchanged, but 60 per cent of the revenue from the tariff is now refunded by Sweden to the Danish producers. Switzerland also gave an informal commitment to increase imports of agricultural products from Denmark, especially cattle for slaughter, meat, and butter.

Much more important to Denmark than the tariff concessions by Great Britain and Sweden were the assurances on behalf of both countries that they would not use support of their domestic agricultures to stimulate production so as to affect Danish exports adversely. In the 1959 Anglo-Danish agreement, the Danes were assured that there was no intention of denying them the opportunity of maintaining their market in the United Kingdom for commodities of concern to them or of sharing in any increase in demand for these products. British policy would be that the production of eggs, milk, and pigmeat in the United Kingdom should become more economic; that the output of eggs should be reduced; and that the milk output should not exceed the requirements of the liquid market, together with a "sufficient reserve."

In reply to the Danish request for an assurance that the removal of the duty on bacon would not be "frustrated" by subsidies, the government, although reserving its right to determine guaranteed prices for pigs with due regard to costs, agreed that subsidy policy should not be used so as to "render nugatory" the opportunities given to Danish producers in the United Kingdom by the removal of the bacon duty.

Within EFTA, much the most important market for Denmark's agricultural exports is, of course, the United Kingdom, and butter and bacon are vastly more important than are any other Danish agricultural exports to the United Kingdom. To appreciate the present situation regarding butter imports into the United Kingdom it is necessary to go back briefly to 1954, when food-rationing and control of food imports in the United Kingdom were ended. From May, 1954, to May, 1958, butter imports into the United Kingdom were unrestricted. Following representations by the New Zealand Government, imports from some countries were restricted from May to December, 1958.

In November, 1961, following another slump in butter prices in the United Kingdom, the government asked all supplying countries to limit their exports until the end of March, 1962; all the suppliers agreed except Ireland, and an antidumping duty of 205 shillings per cwt. was imposed on Irish butter in February, 1962. From April, 1962, imports of butter from all sources were made subject to quotas, and this system is still in force. Since 1967, the imbalance on the world dairy produce market has increased—partly because of subsidized exports from the Common Market countries and partly because former exporters to the Common Market have had to look elsewhere as EEC dairy production has expanded.

Since 1967, the United States has also tightened up its import restrictions, and no new markets have appeared for the low-cost producers—Denmark and New Zealand—although some sales have been made to the small countries in the Far East. (Japan might be expected to become a market for butter, but it continues to maintain tight control of agricultural imports, owing partly to a desire to switch domestic food production from rice to other products.)

A commitment was given by Great Britain to Denmark as part of the EFTA acceleration negotiations in Lisbon in May, 1963, that the butter tariff on non -Commonwealth imports of 15 shillings per cwt. would be suspended as soon as possible. After obtaining agree - ment from Commonwealth suppliers and Ireland, the government removed the tariff on such imports from Denmark on July 10, 1963.

While the quota system remains in force, however, the abolition of the tariff is of minor help to Denmark, since Danish producers cannot increase their sales in Great Britain by reducing prices.

Imports from Denmark have, in fact, remained constant at between
90,000 and 100,000 tons a year since 1960, whereas total U.K. imports
have also remained much the same over this period, although there
have been considerable year-to-year fluctuations. U.K. consumption
has also varied from year to year, largely according to the price of
butter, but does not appear to show any rising trend in the long term.

Most of the import trade in bacon was also in the hands of the
government in Great Britain until 1954. Imports from Denmark and
the Netherlands continued in government hands until November, 1956,
under long-term agreements; in that month, the U.K. Government
ceased to be an importer of bacon. Apart from health regulations,
most other import controls—except those on imports from the Eastern
European countries—were removed in December, 1959. Thus, free
international trade in bacon had only existed for a few years when
EFTA came into existence.

Between 1956 and 1963, especially in the latter part of the period,
there were considerable fluctuations in the price of bacon on the free
market, partly connected with the well-known prewar "pig cycle,"
which still remained in existence. In autumn, 1963, an agreement,
known as the Bacon Market Sharing Understanding, was signed between
Great Britain and the exporting countries—Denmark, Norway, Ireland,
the Netherlands, Poland, and Yugoslavia. The agreement, based on
market shares in the two years immediately preceding, gave U.K.
farmers 36.5 per cent of the U.K. market and Danish farmers 47 per
cent. (The actual allocation during the first year ⌈in tons⌉ was United
Kingdom, 222,400; Denmark, 286,500; Norway, 2,200; Ireland, 27,000;
Netherlands, 13,000; Poland, 18500; Sweden, 10,300; and Yugoslavia,
5,000.)

The object of the Bacon Market Sharing Understanding is to
provide arrangements under which bacon supplies are related to
market needs so that prices are reasonable both to consumers and to
producers. A maximum quantity is determined each year after consultation with the Bacon Market Council, a body that consists of representatives of participating governments under a U.K. chairman, assisted
by trade and industry advisers.

In 1969, negotiations for a renewed agreement for a three-year
period were completed. The revised agreement contains two main
changes. First, there is no longer a specific share of the market for
the U.K. farmer. Instead, the U.K. Government, after consultation
with the Bacon Market Council, decides each year not only the total
quantity of bacon but also the expected level of home production, with

the difference being shared among the exporting countries. Second, the understanding has been strengthened with the object of ensuring that deliveries to the U.K. market are made in a more regular way.

In fact, immediately after the initial agreement was signed in 1963, and again in 1966 and 1967, there was some underfulfillment of quotas, and prices on the U.K. market rose to high levels, so that, at least over part of the period, there has not been pressure by home producers and exporting countries for a larger share of the market.

Since the United Kingdom is by far the largest importer of food in EFTA (indeed, the only large importer), the issue of agricultural trade within EFTA turns largely on Danish food exports to the United Kingdom. In effect, Denmark was promised, when it joined EFTA, that Great Britain would allow it a roughly constant share of the U.K. market, with a prospect of sharing in any rise in U.K. demand.

The outcome may be seen in the trend of total U.K. imports, imports from Denmark, and U.K. production or consumption for five main products. (See Table 21.) Although, as is to be expected with all agricultural products, there are considerable year-to-year fluctuations, it appears that, for butter and bacon, all three (total imports, imports from Denmark, and U.K. consumption or production) have remained at about the same level since the early 1960's. U.K. consumption of cheese and total U.K. imports of cheese show a generally upward trend; imports of cheese from Denmark have on the whole remained static.

With eggs, there has been a marked downward trend both of total U.K. imports and U.K. imports from Denmark, mainly a result of the expansion of domestic production due to the expansion of home production. This, in turn, has been largely a result of more intensive methods of production, but, since eggs are subject to price guarantees and receive an Exchequer subsidy (18 million in 1968-69 and 1969-70), the price stimulus to domestic production must be taken into account. Poultry, however, is not subsidized, and the expansion in domestic production must have been mainly a result of new techniques.

That Denmark and, to a lesser extent, Norway and Portugal have not derived as much benefit from EFTA as have the industrial countries has been recognized by the organization, and there have been a number of attempts to deal with it. The 1968-69 report on EFTA's work states the following:

At their meeting in Stockholm in March 1967, Ministers

TABLE 21

Danish Agricultural Exports to the United Kingdom, 1960–69
(Thousand Tons)

Product	1960	1961	1962	1963	1964	1965	1966	1967	1968	1969
Butter										
U.K. Consumption	429.3	465.1	472.1	459.7	456.8	470.1	481.2	479.8	475.5	476.5
U.K. Imports										
Total	405.3	423.1	406.7	414.2	463.8	439.1	444.4	453.2	440.4	413.3
From Denmark	98.1	93.9	96.0	91.4	90.2	100.6	100.1	95.9	101.6	92.9
Bacon										
U.K. Production (bacon and ham)	180.0	202.0	222.0	217.0	219.0	233.0	206.0	198.0	216.0	233.5
U.K. Imports										
Total	405.4	394.4	398.5	384.9	390.7	397.2	397.0	401.9	405.8	385.7
From Denmark	282.1	280.3	289.1	286.5	290.1	299.5	297.8	300.1	299.5	284.2
Cheese										
U.K. Consumption	231.2	238.2	247.5	247.7	255.1	245.9	255.6	263.9	274.2	280.0
U.K. Imports										
Total	130.0	133.4	138.7	137.7	149.6	149.5	141.2	156.6	177.6	153.7
From Denmark	10.4	10.0	9.2	10.2	9.1	9.3	8.9	9.1	10.7	9.3
Poultry										
U.K. Consumption	292.1	330.1	355.0	357.0	381.0	399.0	427.0	454.0	491.0	546.0[a]
U.K. Imports										
Total	5.6	4.6	4.8	2.3	9.2	12.4	7.8	10.8	7.4	3.9
From Denmark	2.3	1.6	2.6	1.1	8.1	11.7	7.4	10.2	6.7	3.1
Eggs										
U.K. Production (million dozen)	1,080	1,132	1,131	1,197	1,268	1,215	1,255	1,293	1,318	1,247
U.K. Imports (thousand dozen)										
Total	35.1	39.3	24.9	27.9	21.5	22.5	19.8	26.8	20.4	17.2
From Denmark	10.0	8.9	4.4	6.7	3.1	3.0	5.0	7.6	4.5	6.6

aEstimated on per head basis.

held a full discussion on EFTA co-operation in agriculture.
They instructed the Council [the governing body of EFTA]
at official level to carry out a general review of the provisions of the EFTA Convention regarding agriculture, and
to examine whether further steps should be taken to ensure
the satisfactory operation of the provisions. As part of
the work programme established in May 1968, EFTA Ministers agreed to pursue a review, first called for in March
1967, of EFTA co-operation in agriculture and asked Member States to indicate to what extent they could remove,
vis-à-vis their EFTA partners, duties and other obstacles
to trade in Annex D goods. At the Vienna meeting in December 1968 Ministers instructed the Council to continue
the review in the light of statements made by Ministers
during the meeting.

At the Ministerial meeting held in Geneva in May 1969
Ministers had before them a report on the general review
of the agricultural provisions of the EFTA agreement undertaken by the Councils. It appeared during the meeting
that most governments did not consider it constructive to
continue the general discussions on the understanding of
the agricultural provisions in the Convention, but instead
preferred to adopt a more pragmatic approach with regard
to facilitating a further expansion of trade in agricultural
goods within EFTA. Ministers instructed the Councils to
examine the specific steps that might be taken with the aim
of improving trading conditions for agricultural products.
The examination would include dumped and subsidised exports, government support, different price levels for agricultural raw materials and removal of items from Annex
D. A report is to be submitted to Ministers for the next
meeting.[1]

The EFTA Bulletin made the following comments on the work of
the Agricultural Review Committee of EFTA:

In particular, the Committee noted that subsidised exports
from third countries had increased in 1967. It also expressed some concern about the increasing level of govern-
mental support to agriculture in Member countries. The
Committee again agreed that the need to obtain a better
allocation of resources between agriculture and the rest of
the economy remains of fundamental importance to Member
States.[2]

Any further progress regarding agriculture in EFTA, if the EEC is not widened, is likely to be under Article 25, which provides, in brief, that the EFTA Council shall keep the provisions regarding agriculture under review and shall once a year consider the development of trade in agricultural goods within EFTA. There is no reason why there should not be further progress, perhaps on the method adopted by the EEC of package deals, in which concessions by one country in one product or sector are balanced by concessions by another in a different (possibly nonagricultural) sector.

EFTA by itself—and, indeed, even the EEC—however, can make only a limited contribution to multilateral dismantling of agricultural protectionism, which needs to be worldwide and probably must be done through GATT. It is frequently said that, to this end, international commodity agreements are needed, but, in fact, commodity agreements are frequently regarded as devices to raise world market prices to, for example, the EEC level. These questions will be discussed in more detail in Chapter 5.

NOTES

1. EFTA 1968/1969 (Geneva: EFTA, 1969), p. 31.

2. EFTA Bulletin, IX, 8 (November, 1968), p. 20.

4

**AGRICULTURE,
GREAT BRITAIN,
AND THE EEC**

ISSUES IN THE NEGOTIATIONS

Ever since the possibility of British membership in the Common
Market was first seriously raised in 1960, it has been recognized that
the main economic problems of entry were those relating to agriculture, although it is very doubtful that the British side in the first
round of negotiations (1961-63) fully appreciated or even understood
the magnitude and ramifications of the agricultural issues. It is true
that many of the details of the CAP had not then been formulated, but

> it remains odd that the new Minister [of Agriculture—
> Mr. Soames] did not immediately form a much stronger
> EEC section to work on the fundamental agricultural
> problems in anticipation of the decision to apply for
> membership. Nor did the government make any special
> effort to encourage research in this field at universities
> and other non-governmental institutions. This lack of
> preparatory work was to prove a major handicap in 1962.
> Failure to do in good time the detailed preparatory work
> is all the more surprising because in the summer of
> 1961 it was expected that the negotiations would be com-
> pleted and the Treaty ratified during the following year
> so as to make it possible for the EEC to take up formal
> membership of the EEC on 1 January 1963.[1]

In fact, it is extremely doubtful that anyone fully conversant with
the agricultural problem could have predicted that such rapid progress
was possible. The agricultural problem, in a nutshell, is the result
of the different proportion of the working population involved in farming
in Great Britain and in the EEC countries (and the resulting inability

of continental governments to support farm prices other than through
import restrictions). This problem is diminishing as the percentage
of the working population involved in farming declines, so that even
people who are convinced that Great Britain would benefit from membership in the EEC must surely be glad that it did not enter in the
early 1960's.*

During the 1960's, most of the economic research in Great
Britain on the agricultural problems arising from British membership
in the EEC was done jointly by Political and Economic Planning and
the Royal Institute of International Affairs, both of which were heavily
committed to British entry. With the publication in the late 1960's of
some comprehensive studies of EEC farming and the Labour government's White Paper of February, 1970, a more objective view could
be taken.[2]

The agricultural problems inherent in British membership in
the Common Market fall into three groups: the impact on Common-
wealth producers (especially, but by no means exclusively, New
Zealand butter and West Indies sugar producers); the effect on the
British cost of living; and the effect on the U.K. balance of payments.
To some extent, these problems were inherent in the different systems
of agricultural protection that existed in Great Britain and in the six
EEC nations before the Common Market was formed.

These differences had their origin in the last quarter of the nineteenth century, when the progress of the railway, the steamship, and
refrigeration brought cheap cereals and meat to Europe in large
quantities from North and South America and Australasia. The Common Market countries and other continental countries reacted by
raising tariffs to protect their own farmers, whereas Great Britain,
which had abolished the Corn Laws in 1846 and had already gone a
long way toward shifting labor from agriculture to manufacturing,
allowed cheap food to enter freely. As a result, the decline of the
farm population, which is still the center of the farm problem in
continental Western Europe, took place in Great Britain in the nineteenth and early twentieth centuries.

----

*By the same token, it could be argued that, even if the argu-
ments for British entry were strong, it would be desirable to defer
entry until the 1980's. The reply that, if Great Britain does not enter
in the early 1970's, it will never be able to do so is unconvincing to
this author.

Of the European countries, only Denmark reacted by reorganizing its agriculture in such a way as to meet the new competition on equal terms, by switching production from cereals to meat and dairy products and on specialized production—mainly of butter, bacon, and eggs—for the nearby British market, which was growing rapidly both in population and in income per head. Agricultural cooperatives and a high level of general and technical education were also major factors in the economic revolution that had taken place in Danish agriculture by 1914.

Because of their restrictions on food imports, the Common Market countries still had a large proportion of their working population involved in agriculture—varying from 9 per cent in Belgium and 12 per cent in the Netherlands to around 19 per cent in West Germany, 25 per cent in France, and 36 per cent in Italy in the mid-1950's, just before the formation of the Common Market. (See Table 29.) It was therefore impossible for any of these countries, or for the EEC when it was formed, to protect agriculture by means of the producer subsidy system, which was adopted in Great Britain during and after World War II. In 1945, the proportion of the working population involved in farming in Great Britain was already less than 5 per cent.

The traditional British system had the effect of maintaining producer prices and, hence, the volume of domestic production, while avoiding the adverse effects on consumption and also the adverse social effects (that is, the effect on the distribution of real incomes) that result from high food prices. Probably even more important, in view of Great Britain's balance-of-payments difficulties, its position as the largest world importer of many temperate-zone foodstuffs led to low food-selling prices on the domestic market being reflected in low world market prices and, hence, in a reduced import bill. (Under an import levy system, the incentive to agricultural exporting countries to keep down their prices, and perhaps also their costs, is reduced.)

Irrespective of how the EEC agricultural policy later developed, there was, therefore, a serious potential conflict of interest not primarily between British and Common Market farmers (British farmers would probably benefit from higher producer prices, although the extent to which they would do so would depend on market-sharing agreements, which would probably be inevitable), but between joining the Common Market and the desire of British governments to avoid balance-of-payments difficulties, due to higher food import prices, and increases in the cost of living; the latter were likely to result in wage demands and further export difficulties.

The actual development of the CAP, the main details of which were agreed upon in 1962, made the dilemma more acute and more difficult to escape. Under the provisions of the CAP, member countries pay into the common agricultural fund (Fonds Européens d'Orientation et de Garantie Agricole [FEOGA]) the revenue from levies and customs duties on imports from third countries. Since Great Britain would be by far the largest food-importing country, accounting for nearly half the temperate-zone food imports of the enlarged EEC, its contribution would amount to nearly 50 per cent of the total revenue of the fund after the end of the transition period.

These levy payments could be avoided to the extent that British food imports were diverted from third countries to agricultural exporting countries within the EEC; but, since the levy would be determined by the difference between world market and EEC producer prices and since the same factor would determine the additional balance-of-payments cost of buying from the EEC countries rather than from those outside, the balance-of-payments effect could be expected to be equally adverse, whichever course, or whatever gradation of both, was adopted.

At the same time, Great Britain would be the smallest beneficiary from the expenditure side of the common agricultural fund. This expenditure is for three purposes: to support farm prices—by support buying by intervention agencies (the main form of farm price support in the EEC is, of course, the import levies); to reform the structure of agriculture within the EEC; and to subsidize exports to third countries.

Unlike the Netherlands, France, Italy, and West Germany, British exports of foodstuffs are almost negligible in relation to its total exports. Unlike all the existing members of the six EEC nations (although Belgium and the Netherlands to a lesser extent than the other members), British agriculture is in much less need of structural reform, due to the historical developments mentioned above. (The 1960 world census of agriculture showed the average size of agricultural holding to be 47.6 hectares in Great Britain, compared with 6.6 hectares in Belgium, 12.1 hectares in West Germany, and 8.8 hectares in the Netherlands.[3] EEC Commission figures show the average size of farms of one hectare and over in France to be 17.8 hectares. These figures are subject to numerous qualifications, but the point remains.)

West Germany is in a position similar to Great Britain in that it is a large importer of food and exporter of manufactured goods, but it benefits more from the CAP than would Great Britain, due to the higher proportion of its population involved in agriculture (10 per cent compared with 3 per cent in Great Britain), as well as from the greater need for structural reform in agriculture in West Germany— not only compared with Great Britain, but also compared with the other members of the six EEC nations, except Italy. In addition, West Germany has, of course, had a strong balance of payments, which has meant that an exchange deficit through the operation of the CAP would have had little adverse effect on the economic growth rate.

The percentages of the EEC budget that Great Britain is to pay during the transition period, if it enters the EEC, were agreed upon in June, 1971, as follows: 1973, 19.19; 1974, 19.38; 1975, 19.77; 1976, 20.16; and 1977, 20.56. On the assumption that the EEC budget would rise to £1,600 million by 1977, the British contribution in that year would be £ 200 million.[4] For two further years following 1977, the British contribution to the EEC budget would be limited, but

> in 1980 and subsequent years we shall be required to con-
> tribute 90 per cent of our agricultural levy and customs
> duty receipts and such value added tax (VAT) (not
> exceeding the yield of a 1 per cent VAT) as is necessary
> from each member country to close any gap between
> Community expenditure and Community revenues from
> levies and duties.[5]

In this as in other matters, notably New Zealand exports to Great Britain, the negotiations seem to have concentrated on what happens during the transitional period. This is of very minor impor- tance, however, except in the sense that, by 1980, something completely unforeseen may have happened. In addition, there are two crucial considerations that make any calculation centering on Great Britain's contribution to the common agricultural fund, rather than on the balance-of-payments and cost-of-living effects on Great Britain, almost valueless.

First, the income and expenditure of the common agricultural fund are largely the result of other decisions. If the EEC decides to reduce existing producer prices, levy contributions will fall, and vice versa if producer prices are raised. Nor can the expenditure side of the common agricultural fund be determined independently of how much is likely to be available for spending.

Second, as pointed out earlier in this chapter, contributing to the common agricultural fund through import levies and buying from high-cost EEC producing countries, are alternatives for Great Britain if it joins, but the effect of either on the balance of payments would be

identical. At one extreme, Great Britain could reduce its payments
of agricultural levies to the fund to zero by buying all its food from
Western Europe and none from other countries, but there is no reason
to suppose that this would mitigate the balance-of-payments cost of
entry, since the food would be higher priced.

Two other solutions that have sometimes been suggested would
seem to be contrary to the principles of the CAP. One is that New
Zealand and possibly other Commonwealth countries should have
permanent access to the British market on preferential terms—that
is, without paying the EEC import levy, or without paying it in full.
The second possibility is that some of the revenues of the import levies
on food should be retained by Great Britain. Both of these are clearly
ruled out after the end of the transition period, when Great Britain
has said it will accept the basic principles of the CAP.

British negotiators in Brussels are apparently relying on an
escape clause in the Treaty of Rome, to the effect that, if the financial
burdens of entry prove too heavy for a country's economy, they should
be reassessed. Article 105 states that "when a Member State is in
difficulties . . . as regards its balance of payments . . . and when such
difficulties are likely to prejudice the operation of the common market,"
the EEC Commission shall investigate and recommend to the Council
of Ministers "appropriate material assistance," which might include
credit or trade concessions.

Self-evidently, if and when Great Britain is a member of the
EEC, the self-interest of the other member states, if nothing else,
will mean that they will probably be unwilling to envisage a serious
breakdown of the British economy (whatever that may mean). There
is scope, however, for almost unlimited difference of opinion on when
the balance-of-payments burden on Great Britain or on any other
country is unfair or too great. There also seems to be a rather facile
assumption in certain circles in Great Britain that, once Great Britain
is in the Common Market, it can exert a dominating influence on the
development of both the economic and the political policies of the EEC.

THE COSTS OF ENTRY

Several attempts have been made to quantify the likely effects
on the U.K. balance of payments and cost of living if it joins the EEC.
Such attempts can only be very imprecise, but it is nevertheless
essential to make them if an assessment is to be made of the probable
costs and benefits of joining the Common Market. The main difficulty

in making such estimates is that, if the present EEC producer prices were applied to agriculture in Great Britain, Denmark, and Ireland (the latter two countries would certainly join if Great Britain joined), there would be a substantial rise in farm production in these countries.

The extent of the increase would depend on the elasticity of supply of the products that had risen most in price. Some attempts have been made to measure supply elasticities, especially in the United States, where the response of farm production to upward or downward movements in prices is of importance in the government's commodity control scheme.

The difficulties are obvious, however. The response being measured is hypothetical and in the future, and data on historical trends are not of much value.

In addition, technical progress will raise farm output even if prices are stable and if the rate and direction of technical progress is not completely predictable. Also, the extent of the producer price increase in Great Britain, Denmark, and Ireland, if they entered the Common Market, would be so large as to be historically unprecedented; as is clear from the tables in Chapter 1, all meat and cereal prices would rise and the only prices that would fall would be (in Great Britain) those for milk and fruit and vegetables.

In normal circumstances, it might be assumed that the elasticity of supply of agricultural products as a whole in any one country is lower than that of individual farm products, since the total supply of capital and labor in agriculture is in fairly fixed the short term, but the volume of capital and labor devoted to any one farm product is fairly flexible. The technical obstacles to changing from wheat to barley, for example, or from one kind of meat to another are not very great.

If, however, Great Britain, Ireland, and Denmark joined the EEC and existing EEC farm prices were applied, and if no other steps were taken by the authorities (such as fixing production and export shares for the countries concerned), the profitability of farming in these countries would be raised considerably and there might be, if not an actual influx of capital and labor into agriculture, at least a halt to the decline, which has been going on for centuries, in the proportion of the working population employed in agriculture.

To state this possibility is to show how unlikely it is to be acceptable to the six EEC nations. In theory, the resulting increase in production in Great Britain and the other two new member countries could be dealt with by export subsidies on exports to third countries, but it is doubtful that this would be acceptable either to the six EEC nations or to the potential importing countries, who would not welcome the prospect of an increase in dumped imports.

What is likely, in practice, is that, during the course of the negotiations for Great Britain's entry, there will be bargaining not only about prices but also about production shares—that is, the solution is much more likely to be a political one than to depend on the elasticities of supply and demand. Probably the most likely outcome is that EEC producer prices—or prices somewhere between the EEC prices and the present producer prices in Great Britain, Denmark, and Ireland—will be applied to production shares fixed for each country in the enlarged EEC on the basis of actual production in the year or two before the formal entry of Great Britain into the EEC (that is, the year, or two to five years, before 1973 or 1974).

There are several other difficulties in trying to estimate the likely effect of changes in producer prices on production and consumption and of calculating the cost of entry to Great Britain. The response of farmers to higher prices depends partly on how long they think these prices are going to last. If the EEC appears likely to bring about reductions in producer prices, the increase in production in the three applicant countries will be less than otherwise. On the consumption side, there are likely to be sharp switches in consumption away from products that have risen in price, particularly butter, cheese, beef, and (to a smaller extent) bacon, pork, and poultry, although, in the longer run, these will be offset to some extent by increases in real income.

One of the main imponderables in calculating Great Britain's contribution by means of levies to the common agricultural fund is the relative future course of EEC and world prices. If, for example, because of rising world population, more rapid increase in income per head in the underdeveloped countries, or larger imports of food by China and the Soviet bloc, the balance of world supply and demand for temperate-zone foodstuffs changed and world prices rose nearer to the EEC level, the levy contribution would be smaller, even if Great Britain continued to buy large quantities of foodstuffs from third countries.

Although any or all of these are long-term possibilities, there is little prospect of their making any appreciable difference in the forseeable future. A 1970 FAO study estimated that the underdeveloped

countries would become small net exporters of grain by 1985 and
small net importers of beef.[6] (Their trade in other meats, and dairy
products, is very small.) Three major variables are involved in this
kind of prediction, each of which is subject to very large, and to some
extent unpredictable, changes—the rate of population growth, growth
in income per head, and growth in productivity in agriculture in the
underdeveloped countries. The net outcome of these factors is
uncertain, so the only safe course seems to be to assume a rough
continuance of present and past trends, unless there are good reasons
to the contrary.

In this respect, probably the most useful single indicator is the
trend in the price of wheat during the 1960's. There was an upswing
in world wheat prices in 1961 under the influence of the Canadian
drought and large Chinese wheat purchases. Further price increases
took place in 1963-66, as a result of Soviet crop failures. With record
world crops in 1966—67, however, prices began to fall, and they continued to fall until the end of the decade.

The British Government White Paper of July, 1971, laid considerable emphasis on the rise in world food prices since the publication of the previous White Paper (by the Labour government) in
February, 1970. (It stated that "earlier estimates of our levy receipts
[sic] in the mid-1970s have already been invalidated by the recent substantial narrowing of the gap between world and Community food
prices."[7])

This is clearly too short a period on which to base any longer-
term predictions, however, and the rise in world prices during 1970
and 1971 was to a considerable extent due to two identifiable and presumably nonrecurring factors—a drought in New Zealand in 1970, which
affected beef and dairy produce prices, and a reduction in U.S. production of maize (due to leaf blight), which had repercussions on the
prices of other cereals.[8]

Although the effect on cost of living is popularly regarded as
the most serious problem arising from British entry into the Common
Market, there is no doubt that, as far as Great Britain is concerned,
the balance-of-payments problem is more serious; for it has been the
balance-of-payments problem that has retarded British economic
growth since the end of World War II. An attempt to estimate the
balance-of-payments effect is somewhat confused because it may
take any one of three forms.

First, if Great Britain continues to buy large quantities of food

from nonmembers of the enlarged EEC, it will take the form of a pay-
ment of levies (constituting the difference between the world market
price and the EEC price) into the common agricultural fund. Second,
at the opposite extreme, Great Britain might decide to reduce its
imports from third countries substantially and also to increase substantially its purchase of food from within the enlarged EEC. In this
case, payments into the common agricultural fund would be much
smaller than in the first case, but the effect on the U.K. balance of
payments would be equally severe, since higher prices would be paid
for food imports.

Third, it might be possible, through agreements with the non-
EEC food-exporting countries, to induce them to raise their prices
nearer to the EEC level. This, in fact, is what has been done in the
1970-71 negotiations regarding exports to Great Britain of New
Zealand butter and cheese. Quantities of butter and cheese exported
to Great Britain are to be reduced over the transition period, but the
prices to be paid to New Zealand are to be the average of the four
years 1969-72, which was higher than the prices in the preceding
years.

Under this arrangement, New Zealand will be better off and the
receipts of the common agricultural fund will be lower than under an
arrangement whereby quantities of butter and cheese imported by
Great Britain from New Zealand would be reduced and prices received
by New Zealand would remain the same. The effect on the British
balance of payments, however, will be no different from what it would
be regarding these two commodities if one of the first two solutions
were adopted.

The total effect on the balance of payments of U.K. entry into
the Common Market is, therefore, easier to calculate than is the
likely British contribution to the common agricultural fund. The net
effect of the agricultural changes on the U.K. balance of payments is
basically a function of the difference between world market and EEC
prices, multiplied by the quantities imported by Great Britain from
non-EEC sources before entry.

There are three uncertainties in the calculation: the future
course of world market prices, the future course of EEC producer
prices (which are likely to be lower in the Community of Ten [the
EEC plus Britain, Ireland, Denmark, and Norway] than in the Community of six [the present EEC], since Great Britain, Denmark, and
Ireland are low-cost producers), and the extent to which retail price
increases will lead to reduced consumption, and hence reduced

imports, in Great Britain of products that have risen in price. Although these uncertainties are substantial, they are less than the uncertainties attending a calculation of payments by Great Britain into the common agricultural fund, at least after the transition period. (During the transition period, the payments would apparently be determined by an arbitrary formula.)

A rough estimate might be made for dairy products, as follows. For these, producer prices in the EEC are usually (taking the average of 1955-71) about twice as high as the cost, insurance, and freight (c.i.f.) import price in Great Britain from the main supplying countries—New Zealand and Denmark. Total U.K. imports of these products in 1969 were $420 million, or £175 million. Since only some $20 million, or 7 per cent, of these came from high-cost EEC sources, it may be assumed that the balance-of-payments cost, in the form of either levy payments or higher import prices or some combination of the two, would be an additional 90 per cent of £175 million, or about £157 million. This would be mitigated to the extent that butter consumption in Great Britain was reduced by higher prices (itself a loss in welfare) and to the extend that existing EEC producer prices were reduced.

It is difficult to believe, however, that the balance-of-payments cost on dairy products alone could be much less than £100 million, and, at a rough guess, as far as can be predicted on the basis of estimating conditions, it seems unlikely that the total balance-of-payments cost on foodstuffs could be less than £400 million or £500 million. Given that there have been only a few years since World War II in which Great Britain has achieved a balance-of-payments current-account surplus of this order (notably 1970 and 1971, when the cost in deflationary measures and low economic growth was very high), the seriousness of the problem does not need emphasis.

A PROPOSAL FOR THE
TRANSITION PERIOD

The question of whether, and how, the adverse effects of the CAP on Great Britain might be reduced by policy changes by the British Government will now be examined. As mentioned in Chapter 3, the 10 per cent duty on bacon and the duty on tinned pork (which ranged from 5 to 10 per cent) were removed in two stages during 1960-61. Several other food products, which either are or could be imported by Great Britain from Denmark, are still subject to tariffs, however. A case can be made for removing these not only on grounds of equity (since Denmark has not gained reciprocal advantages under the EFTA agreement), but also because and increase in food imports from Denmark, as well as from Ireland, would be an advantage to Great Britain during the transition period in the payments problem that will arise if the negotiations are successful.

At present, these tariffs include the following:

Dairy Products

milk and cream (fresh)—10 per cent

milk (condensed)

whole unsweetened—30 pence per cwt.
whole sweetened—38 pence per cwt.
skimmed—10 per cent

milk powder—30 pence per cwt.

eggs (in shell)—5-9 pence per 120, depending on size

Meat

beef and veal (canned)

jellied veal—10 per cent
other—18 per cent

poultry

Fresh, chilled, frozen, or canned—1 pence per lb.
salted, smoked, or dried—10 per cent

Most of these products are of minor importance in the present pattern of U.K. food imports from Denmark; however, even though imports of certain products are small, this does not mean that they would remain small if obstacles to trade were removed. Also there may be scope for trade where it is presently nonexistent, as in liquid milk. Trade in poultry, which has been reduced to negligible proportions, partly because of a quota on imports into Great Britain, might be revived, as might trade in eggs.

There would not be any practical difficulties in increasing imports into Great Britain of the main Danish export products—butter and bacon—even though the import trade is in private hands, since both commodities are subject to quotas, the former determined by the British Government and the latter established after consultation with the various interests involved under the Bacon Market Sharing Understanding. Imports of the largest variety of cheese consumed in Great Britain—cheddar—have also been subject to quotas since 1969, although the main variety of cheese of interest to Denmark—blue-veined—is unregulated. For most other food imports, the abolition of British tariffs on Danish food imports would constitute a simple way of encouraging imports from Denmark.

Such a move would be quite compatible with the GATT regulations, which forbid reduction or removal of tariffs from any one country (except on a nondiscriminatory basis) under the misleadingly named Most-Favored Nation Principle, unless the removal is part of the formation of a customs union or a free trade area. Imports from Ireland already have free entry to Great Britain under the Anglo-Irish Free Trade Agreement of December, 1965, but there is probably also scope for increasing the imports to Great Britain from Ireland of the products that are subject to quotas—mainly bacon and butter.

At the end of the transition period, there will be a considerable shift in domestic agricultural production from meat and dairy products to cereals, because cereals prices will rise more. (An incidental effect of the rise in cereals prices and hence of animal foodstuffs will be to reduce the price advantage that intensive methods of production of eggs and poultry and, to some extent, lambs and calves have over older methods. The increase in output of eggs and poultry in Great Britain has been largely due to more intensive production methods, which are prohibited by law in Denmark. It may be impracticable to prohibit intensive farming in Great Britain and in other countries, for economic reasons, but many people would regard with satisfaction an economic arrangement that tilted the balance in favor of the less intensive older methods.)

Such a shift would, in any case, be rational in an enlarged EEC because Great Britain's efficiency advantage over the six EEC nations is greatest in cereals, which, in turn, results from the link between larger farms and efficiency being closer in cereals than in other agricultural products. An optimum pattern of agricultural support in Great Britain from the balance-of-payments standpoint would also involve a shift in this direction. An increase in imports of dairy products and meat from Denmark would, therefore, be advantageous to Great Britain from this point of view also.

LOW-COST FARM PRODUCTION WITHIN
THE ENLARGED EEC

On the assumption that the negotiations that began in June, 1970, are successful and that Denmark, Norway, and Ireland join the Common Market at the same time as Great Britain does, the enlarged EEC will contain three low-cost producing countries—Denmark, Ireland, and Great Britain—with the other members all being high-cost producers of most temperate-zone foodstuffs other than fruit and vegetables. The total farm output of the three low-cost producing countries in 1967 was $3,470 million, equivalent to 14.3 per cent of the total farm output of the six EEC nations.

If an expansion in agricultural output in the three low-cost producing countries were politically feasible immediately before, and during, the transition period, how much effect could it have on the agricultural problems facing Great Britain if the negotiations are successful—that is, in alleviating the cost-of-living and balance-of-payments problems? As noted earlier, the two are inextricably connected, and anything that contributes to the solution of the first will automatically help the second.

Table 22 provides a picture of the share of low-cost producing countries within the enlarged EEC for their main commodities, using 1968 production figures. On the basis of these 1968 production figures, the share of the low-cost producing countries in the total production of the enlarged EEC would be (in percentage terms) butter, 19; cheese, 12; milk, 20; beef, 26; mutton, 56; pigmeat, 22; poultry, 25; and eggs, 28.

To see what effect an expansion of production in Great Britain, Denmark, and Ireland would have on internal prices (producer and retail) within the enlarged EEC, it is necessary to compare production in the low-cost producing countries with consumption, not production, in the enlarged EEC. It is, therefore, necessary to take the preceding figures in conjunction with self-sufficiency figures for the enlarged EEC. (See Table 23. Figures of self-sufficiency for the six EEC nations are also given, although these are not directly relevant to the present argument.)

In cases where the three low-cost producers make up a large share of the total production of the enlarged EEC and, in addition, where the enlarged EEC would be fairly self-sufficient (in other words, where the low-cost producers contribute a large proportion

TABLE 22

Share of Low-Cost Agricultural Producing
Countries in Enlarged EEC
(Thousand Metric Tons)

Product	Total Community of Ten	Great Britain	Denmark	Ireland
Butter	1,514	54	160	78
Cheese	2,268	120	106	29
Liquid milk	104,303	12,478	5,122	3,675
Beef and veal	5,839	935	247	337
Mutton and lamb	543	251	3	48
Pigmeat	7,105	837	739	123
Poultry	23,331	5,040	650	260
Hen eggs	35,734	8,772	857	419

Source: FAO, Production Yearbook, 1969 (Rome, 1970).

of the consumption of the enlarged EEC), it may be assumed that a
further expansion of output in the low-cost producing countries would
have a fairly substantial impact on prices within the enlarged EEC.

The first condition is, however, met only in mutton, which, it
is recognized, will not present any serious problems (both production
and consumption are very low in the six EEC nations). Expansion of
production of beef, poultry, and eggs by the low-cost producers, who
presently account for one-quarter of total production in the ten countries of the enlarged EEC, might also mitigate price rises. In butter,
cheese, and pigmeat, where their share of production is only about
one-fifth, a further expansion of production would have only a small
impact.

The most serious problems for Great Britain are likely to be
in the sphere of butter, cheese, and pigmeat—that is, the commodities
where the low-cost producers will have the smallest share of production of the enlarged EEC. A concerted effort toward expansion of

TABLE 23

Degree of EEC Self-Sufficiency in Community
of Ten and Community of Six, 1965/66

Product	Community of Ten	Community of Six
Butter	84	102
Cheese	96	99
Beef	90	84
Pigmeat	103	98
Wheat	94	110
Feed grains	73	71

Source: "Current Notes on the European Source Community,"
European Community Information Service, No. 1 (May, 1968), p. 28.

output of these products in the United Kingdom and of U.K. imports
of these products from Denmark and Ireland in the years before
EEC entry might have gone some way toward mitigating the effect of
entry on the U.K. cost of living, but it is doubtful that such a measure
will be politically practicable after January, 1973 (if the United Kingdom
enters on that date). Also, a deliberate expansion of production in
these countries would have to be by means of higher producer prices,
so the advantages of expansion would be smaller than they appear to
be at first sight.

The possibilities of mitigating the balance-of-payments and
cost-of-living effects on Great Britain if it enters the EEC, by means
of increasing output in Great Britain, Denmark, and Ireland, are now
rather small. Even if they were large, the effects of British entry
on world agriculture generally (by reducing exports and incomes in
the low-cost non-European exporting countries) and on the allocation
of resources in the producing and consuming countries would be very
serious.

WORLD TRADE IF GREAT BRITAIN ENTERS EEC

The products and areas that are most "at risk" if Great Britain
joins the EEC are indicated by Tables 24 and 25, which show U.K.

imports by commodity groups and U.K. imports from non-EEC sources in 1969. To show the effect of the enlarged EEC on international trade, it is obviously necessary to consider, in addition, the total imports, and how much is from EEC and non-EEC sources of the existing members of the EEC, which are also shown in Tables 24 and 25. Finally, to obtain an indication of the importance of the United Kingdom and the EEC (both together and separately) in world trade, Table 26 provides figures for the imports, by commodity groups, of the other two major importing areas, the United States and Japan.

Total U.K. food imports from countries other than the six EEC nations totaled $3,727 million in 1969—equal to nearly two-thirds of the total food imports from non-EEC sources of the six EEC nations, $6,041 million—despite the much larger population of the EEC countries, 84 million, compared with 54 million in the United Kingdom. Apart from Denmark (and the other EFTA countries) and Ireland, both of which are fairly certain to join the EEC if Great Britain does and both of whose food exports to Great Britain will therefore not be disrupted, the major sources of British food imports were New Zealand, with more than $425 million of food exports to the United Kingdom; Canada, the United States, and Australia, all with more than $200 million; the Union of South Africa, with just under $200 million; and the Central and South American countries, whose total exports amounted to over $400 million.

In terms of commodities, the bulk of U.K. food imports consisted of meat, butter, wheat, maize, fruit, vegetables, and sugar. A detailed commodity-by-country examination of non-European food exports to the United Kingdom, and the risk to this trade if Great Britain joins the EEC, will not be undertaken here, as the salient facts are well known. Fruit and vegetable trade is not likely to be greatly affected, since EEC producers are competitive with others and since world trade (including present U.K. imports) is carried on mainly on the basis of comparative efficiency. The crucial items are New Zealand dairy products; South American meat and cereals; cereals from Australia, Canada, and the United States; and sugar from the West Indies, Mauritius, and Australia.

Although the probable effects on individual countries and commodities are not discussed in great detail here, it is useful to speculate on the probable impact on total world trade in the main commodity groups. Table 26 shows that the United Kingdom is at present a much larger importer of meat and of dairy products than are the six EEC nations and, in fact, is a much larger importer of dairy products than are the other three major importing areas (the six EEC

TABLE 24

EEC and U.K. Food Imports, by Commodity Groups, 1969
(Thousand $)

SITC Group	EEC		United Kingdom	
	From World	From EEC	From World	From EEC
001 Live animals	707,696	324,613	129,274	2,767
011 Meat (fresh, chilled, or frozen)	1,265,749	704,521	553,376	8,738
011.1 Meat of bovine animals (fresh, chilled, or frozen)	573,372	303,034	239,355	7,835
011.2 Meat of sheep and goats (fresh, chilled, or frozen)	46,645	19,820	223,476	133
011.3 Meat of swine (fresh, chilled, or frozen)	311,064	221,541	13,780	14
011.4 Poultry (fresh, chilled, or frozen)	172,623	139,255	2,466	19
012 Meat (dried, salted, or smoked)	19,571	16,477	307,538	7,991
022 Milk and cream	211,461	204,852	25,311	4,457
023 Butter	108,743	105,338	308,191	13,960
024 Cheese and curd	333,790	252,567	96,309	15,270
025 Eggs	118,097	99,153	11,910	908
031 Fish (fresh, chilled, or frozen)	233,390	83,859	55,233	6,065
041 Wheat (unmilled)	599,263	314,463	317,811	85,238
043 Barley (unmilled)	247,037	195,097	35,178	1,928
044 Maize (unmilled)	638,493	133,007	188,060	37,715
048 Cereal preparations and preparations of flour or fruit and vegetables	140,289	123,112	17,030	7,733
051 Fruit (fresh) and nuts	1,250,981	395,218	350,987	51,099
054 Vegetables, nuts, and tubers (fresh or dried)	813,932	466,656	221,514	65,343
061 Sugar and honey	202,677	103,036	266,328	5,611

Source: OECD, Foreign Trade Statistics, "Series B" (Paris, annual publication).

TABLE 25

EEC and U.K. Food Imports,
by Country of Origin, 1969
(SITC Division O, "Food and Live Animals")
(Thousand $)

Country	United Kingdom	EEC
World	4,200,647	10,511,339
EEC	473,682	4,470,708
Non-EEC	3,726,965	6,040,631
Canada	229,222	122,977
United States	215,973	860,967
Japan	54,872	58,126
EFTA	535,213	646,531
Sino-Soviet bloc	164,557	622,777
Less-developed countries	1,064,137	2,913,107
Africa	349,925	1,053,970
Central and South America	409,046	1,526,158
Far East	211,463	235,482
Near East	93,703	97,497
Australia/New Zealand/		
Union of South Africa	898,694	177,264
Australia	283,151	72,647
New Zealand	425,309	13,292
Union of South Africa	190,234	91,325
Denmark	408,603	254,545
Ireland	321,138	22,986

Source: OECD, Foreign Trade Statistics, "Series B" (Paris, annual publication).

nations, the United States, and Japan) added together, while its meat purchases are equivalent to 70 per cent of total imports by the other areas. U.K. imports of cereals are about two-thirds those of the EEC and are also less than those of Japan. U.K. imports of fruit and vegetables are larger than those of the United States but less than those of the EEC, and U.K. imports of sugar are about the same as those of the EEC but only about 40 per cent of those of the United States.

TABLE 26

Food Imports by the United Kingdom, the EEC, the United States, and Japan, 1969
(Million $)

SITC	United Kingdom	EEC[a]	United States	Japan
00 Live animals	129	383	119	14
01 Meat and meat preparations	1,038	449	864	164
02 Dairy products and eggs	442	110	75	42
03 Fish and fish preparations	168	341	692	202
04 Cereals and cereal preparations	605	978	55	861
05 Fruit and vegetables	860	1,548	662	274
06 Sugar preparations and honey	270	285	708	251
07 Tea, coffee, cocoa, and spices	438	151	1,268	124
08 Animal foodstuffs	195	729	69	103
Total	4,201	6,040	4,531	2,055
Total excluding sugar preparations and honey, as well as tea, coffee, cocoa, and spices	3,493	5,604	2,555	1,680

aImports from non-EEC countries.

Source: OECD, Foreign Trade Statistics, "Series B" (Paris, annual publication).

These figures again indicate the key importance of dairy products and meat in the effect of British entry into the EEC on world trade, although these over-all figures naturally conceal many important effects on individual countries and subgroups of commodities. (The over-all totals for fruit and vegetables and sugar mean little, owing to the heterogeneous nature of the first two and the links of major importing countries with particular exporting countries in all three.)

PAST AND PRESENT OBJECTIVES OF
BRITISH FARMING POLICY

To what extent will acceptance of the Common Market's agricultural policy represent a break in British policies in relation to both domestic agricultural production and foreign purchase? Great Britain was a free trade country for agriculture, as for manufactured goods, until the Depression during the 1930's, and, with the exception of sugar beet, which was subsidized from 1925 onward, domestic production was unsubsidized, so that the level both of home production and imports was determined by the free market. In 1932, duties and import quotas were imposed on several agricultural products at the same time as tariffs were imposed on manufactured goods.

The major impetus to home production, however, came during World War II, when saving shipping space was considered vital. The expansion was mainly in cereals production, which rose by about 70 per cent; many livestock were slaughtered, and total farm output rose by only 20 per cent. The price guarantees and support arrangements that came into force during the war were continued with the Agriculture Act of 1947, which also provided for an annual review. This, together with the Agriculture Acts of 1957, 1964, and 1967, is the basis of postwar British agricultural policy.

During the postwar years, the dollar shortage dominated economic policy, and further efforts were made to expand agricultural output, which rose by another 20 per cent between 1946-47 and 1951-52. Food rations were more stringent than they had been during the war years; bread was unrationed throughout the war but was rationed from July, 1946, to May, 1949.

Agricultural policy during the postwar period may be divided into three distinct periods: up to 1954, when the emphasis was on expansion of home production for balance-of-payments reasons; 1954-64, when the balance-of-payments problem receded somewhat and the fall in world prices of food and raw materials made expansion of domestic agriculture less attractive; and the period from 1964 onward, when the balance of payments was again dominant and "selective expansion" was the order of the day.

During this period, there were some changes in the strategy of agricultural policy, but these were less important than were the changes in over-all objectives just referred to. By 1961, increasing imports and declining world market prices caused Exchequer support to grow. It reached a peak of £343 million in 1961-62. By 1969-70, the figure was £280 million, even though prices had risen by some 34 per cent in the intervening years.

The fall does not, however, mean that the total of government support to agriculture had fallen; in the meantime, there had been a shift from Exchequer support to import controls, and, indeed, the volume of home production and Great Britain's self-sufficiency ratios for the main agricultural products indicate that there was probably a rise in the degree of state support.

Apart from horticulture, which had always been supported by tariffs rather than by deficiency payments, butter was the first major agricultural product to be regulated by import controls. Butter quotas were imposed temporarily for a few months in 1958 and were made permanent in March, 1962. In 1964, under the "Soames Plan," agreements on minimum import prices were reached with supplying countries for wheat, barley, beef, and pork, and, in the same year the Bacon Market Sharing Understanding was inaugurated.

The National Plan, published in September, 1965, forecast an extra demand by 1970 of some 200 million of temperate-zone foodstuffs and proposed a selective expansion program to help reduce imports.

In those commodities such as eggs, poultry and maincrop potatoes where the United Kingdom is already virtually self-sufficient, the need will be to meet increasing demand during the plan period. . . . Meat will have one of the most important parts to play in any selective expansion programme. Mutton and lamb and pigmeat can make a substantial contribution to our increasing requirements consistently with our commitments to our overseas suppliers, but the main emphasis must be on the expansion of beef and veal production which will have to be increased to the full extent of the technical possibilities. This will in turn entail an expansion in milk production,

which will meet the growing consumption of liquid milk
and cream and a substantial part of our additional requirements in milk products. The expansion of meat and milk
production will increase considerably the demand for
cereal feed and, consistently with our international commitments, a substantial part of the additional requirement
should come from home sources. . . . In all, the Government would expect home agriculture to be able to meet a
major part of the additional demand expected by 1970.[9]

Although the National Plan was formally abandoned in July, 1966, the
section dealing with agriculture was not discarded, and, indeed, the
production targets for 1970 were, in the main, reached.

The growth in agricultural self-sufficiency during the years
since 1945 and in comparison with the prewar period is illustrated in
Table 27. For all three main groups of products—milk products,
meat, and grains—there has been a steady trend toward greater self-
sufficiency in Great Britain. The self-sufficiency ratio grew from
31 per cent before World War II to 49 per cent in 1968-69 for milk
products (for liquid milk, it has always been 100 per cent); for meat,
from 47 per cent to 69 per cent; and for grains, from 31 per cent to
60 per cent in 1969-70.

The trend has varied from product to product; for example, in
grains, there have been marked divergences at times in the movement
of the ratio for the two main products, wheat and barley. The ratio
for meat in 1968-69 was, in fact, rather lower than had been the case
during the immediately preceding years, due to the outbreak of foot
and mouth disease in autumn, 1968.

It is not possible to say exactly how much of this growth in
self-sufficiency has been due to government policy. Where there is
no subsidy or guaranteed prices and/or where home production has
increased over the years despite a reduction in the guaranteed price,
it is safe to say that there have been autonomous factors on the supply
side making for increased production. Probably the main products
where this has been true are poultry and eggs. For most other products, it can be assumed that the growth of home production and,
hence, self-sufficiency has in the main been due to deliberate government policy.

AGRICULTURE'S IMPORT-SAVING ROLE

The report by the Economic Development Committee (EDC) for

TABLE 27

U.K. Self-Sufficiency Ratios, Prewar to 1969/70
(Home Production As Percentage of Total Supplies)

Product	Prewar Average	1946/47	1959/60	1963/64	1968/69	1969/70
Wheat	23	26	37	60	43	42
Barley	46	95	89	94	97	90
All grains	31	59	53	56	61	60
Beef and veal	49	59	64	73	77	77
Mutton and lamb	36	24	40	43	42	40
Pork	78	34	94	98	98	101
Bacon and ham	29	36	33	36	35	38
Poultry	80	72	97	99	99	100
All meat	47	45	61	68	69	—
Butter	8	8	7	8	11	12
Cheese	24	9	40	43	40	45
All milk products	31	19	44	44	49	—
Eggs (in shell)	—	—	98	97	100	99

Source: Great Britain, Annual Review and Determination of Guarantees, Cmnd. 4623 (London: HMSO,

Agriculture, entitled <u>Agriculture's Import-Saving Role</u> and published in July, 1968, was a landmark in the development of agricultural policy.[10] Its main conclusions were that it would be possible to raise gross farm output by £345 million (about 17 per cent) and net output by about £185 million (or 22 per cent) over 1967-68 levels by 1972-73, with further "consequential increases" thereafter; that the net import saving of this expansion would be about £220 million a year on completion of the expansion; that the costs of the expansion would be £230 million in capital assets (buildings, equipment, machinery, and drainage, plus lime); and that the additional cost of other physical inputs (fertilizer, feed, sprays, fuel and power, machinery repairs, and the like) should build up to about £110 million a year on completion of the expansion.

Cereals production, according to the EDC, would increase by 3.5 million tons over 1967-68 figures. In the livestock sector, the main increases (over 1967), in rounded terms, would be milk (280 gallons), beef and veal (160,000 tons), pork (135,000 tons), bacon (170,000 tons), and poultry (155,000 tons), although much of the beef would not be obtained until after 1972-73.

The broad objectives of the EDC report were accepted by the British Government, although it did not commit itself to production targets for particular commodities. Speaking on the government's response to the report in the House of Commons on November 12, 1968, the minister of agriculture said that, although "the full import saving envisaged by the Committee would not be reached by 1972-73, nevertheless, by that time, we should achieve a net saving of about £160 million a year."[11]

Speaking to the Farmers' Club the next day, the minister went into the then government's attitude on particular commodities in more detail:

<u>Milk and beef.</u> Our broad aim is an increase in the output of beef and milk similar to that suggested by the EDC.

<u>Cereals.</u> We want to increase production as much as is technically possible. This may not be as rapid as the Little Neddy assumed but it should still enable us fully to meet the growing requirements of feed for the expanding livestock population.

<u>Pigmeat.</u> We have been self-sufficient for pork for many years. It is our intention that this should continue. Now

that pigs are becoming more plentiful I hope we shall see
an expansion in our bacon production.

Mutton and lamb. We are not aiming to increase mutton
and lamb production.

The 1970 Annual Review White Paper showed that selective expansion
was still the watchword:

Selective expansion is still needed. It is needed not only
to save imports now but if we go into the EEC to reduce
the bill which would have to be paid through adoption of
the common agricultural policy. The aim is for agriculture to produce more of the right commodities to meet
rising demand on an economic basis. The priority products are still beef, pigmeat, wheat and barley.[12]

Following the change of government in June, 1970, it was
announced in October of that year that there would be a further change-
over from deficiency payments to import levies for the basic farm
products. Levies were introduced in 1971 for beef and veal, mutton
and lamb, and milk products other than butter and cheese. The government also announced its intention of phasing out the deficiency payments
on eggs and raising "significantly" the minimum import price for
eggs.[13] The aims of the policy, as distinct from its method of implementation, remain unchanged:

A rising trend in production is . . . of particular importance in connection with possible entry into the EEC.

The government have decided to make determina-
tions which will, generally speaking, maintain the existing
balance of agricultural production and will, taking into
account the October adjustments, meet the increased
costs on most of the major guaranteed commodities
fully.[14]

THE DEBATE ON EXPANDING
DOMESTIC PRODUCTION

Since the policy of expanding agriculture for balance-of-payments
reasons was adopted just after World War II, there has been a continuing
debate among economists about its economic effects and justification.
The debate was inaugurated with a series of articles in the Economic

Journal in 1950 and 1951 and has continued ever since.[15] It has been inconclusive, and some of the key factors that have to be taken into consideration are almost impossible to quantify.

One of the arguments most frequently used in the past for agricultural support was that it provided agriculture with equivalent protection to that provided to manufacturing by means of tariffs. This view has lost much of its force, however, now that tariffs on manufactured imports have been substantially reduced through GATT negotiations.

When the agricultural expansion program was initiated during the postwar years, there was a widespread belief that Great Britain's balance-of-payments problem would be a continuing one (which has turned out to be accurate) and also that there would be a long-term trend for world food prices to rise due to population increases and industrialization in the underdeveloped countries and in the agricultural exporting countries.

The latter assumption has turned out to be unwarranted, because productivity in agriculture has risen more rapidly than in industry. Although a rise in world market prices of food remains a long-term possibility—for example, if the Soviet Union and China became large food importers—it seems unwise to base present policy on a hypothetical possibility that has often been predicted but has never come about.

One of the main problems in the balance-of-payments case for expanding agricultural production in Great Britain has been that an increase in domestic production of meat and dairy products leads to an increase in imports of cereals for use as animal foodstuffs. According to the EDC report mentioned above, the expansion in livestock production postulated would call for an increase in the supply of feed grain of about 2.5 million tons over the 1967-68 figure of 22.7 million tons.[16]

A theoretically optimum degree of agricultural expansion (from this limited viewpoint) would probably involve expanding cereals production in Great Britain more than meat and dairy products production and would, therefore, involve changes in the relative producer prices of the two groups of products, presumably by means of import levies. Such a change would also encourage more efficient utilization of domestic grass for livestock feeding. Such a policy would reduce imports of cereals but would maintain outlets in Great Britain for countries that are low-cost meat and dairy producers.

There are two other major imponderables in the import-saving argument. First, adherents of the policy of expanding domestic agriculture have tended to take a very pessimistic view of the possibilities of expanding British exports, by devaluation or by any other means, and have, therefore, looked on import-saving as almost the only way out of the balance-of-payments problem. (This broadly, is the view taken by E. A. G. Robinson.) In other words, they have assumed that the elasticity of demand for British exports is low.

There is, however, no obvious reason why this should be so. The elasticity of demand for a particular country's exports will be low if it already supplies a large part of world imports. This was the case, for example, with British industrial exports in the first half of the nineteenth century, when Great Britain was the only industrialized country. In these circumstances, British exports could only rise substantially as a result of rising world demand, and not by increasing their share of world exports at the expense of other industrial exporting countries.

There is now a large and increasing number of industrial countries competing in world trade, however, and a devaluation by any one of them is likely to give a substantial boost to its exports. The results of the 1967 devaluation by Great Britain tends to confirm this fairly optimistic view of the elasticity of demand for industrial exports.

The second factor (which was ignored in the EDC report) is the reciprocity effect on British exports if, as a result of expanding domestic agricultural production, British agricultural imports are reduced. An attempt to estimate the reciprocity effects of the expansion proposed by the EDC on six overseas agricultural exporting countries (Argentina, Australia, New Zealand, the Union of South Africa, Denmark, and Ireland) concluded that British exports to these countries could fall by £92 million if the import-saving projections of the EDC report were fulfilled.[17] This sum would have to be deducted from the EDC's figure of some £220 million net import saving (£256 million gross—that is, ignoring the increased imports of inputs). Obviously, the methodology of this kind of calculation is debatable. (It is not clear, for example, whether an increase in British food imports from these countries would have the reverse effect.)

The past controversy over agricultural import saving will become largely irrelevant if Great Britain enters the Common Market, for it will have to adopt the producer prices prevailing in the six EEC nations or something rather lower but still considerably above the present

U.K. producer prices (except for liquid milk, which is higher in price in the United Kingdom. If entry into the EEC were regarded as probable, it would have been rational for Great Britain to move domestic producer prices gradually upward in the years preceding entry and to accept the resulting increase in production (which would itself reduce the balance-of-payments problem arising from entry), particularly for products where there is at present a large gap.

This, together with an increase in imports from Denmark and Ireland, would have provided some degree of insurance against balance-of-payments difficulties (the large retail price increases) after Great Britain joined. The criteria that have in the past been used to try to decide whether or not the U.K. agricultural policy is rational in the present international trade context would no longer apply if Great Britain could not import cheap temperate-zone food from Australasia, South America, and other non-European sources on its present scale.

That so much doubt and dispute have arisen about the economic rationality of the British agricultural import-saving program over the years 1945-70, however, is by implication a serious reflection on the policies likely to be adopted if Great Britain joins the EEC, which will make the previous agricultural expansion program look extremely modest and moderate by comparison. The reciprocity effect on U.K. exports of reduced U.K. imports of food from the Commonwealth countries will —if the approach in the study just cited is correct —lead to a much greater drop in U.K. exports of manufactured goods to the Commonwealth countries than has the agricultural import-saving program hitherto.[18]

This will not be offset by increased U.K. exports to the countries of Western Europe if it buys more food from them, since the reciprocity argument in relation to the Commonwealth countries is based on the fact that, in many cases, the United Kingdom takes a large proportion of their total exports, and hence U.K. imports from them have a dominating effect on their balances of payments.

This does not apply in relation to the agricultural exporting countries of Western Europe, whose total exports are much more diversified both in terms of product and of country of destination. Also, if domestic agricultural expansion in the United Kingdom has already been carried—as many economists believe—beyond the point where the additional domestic economic resource costs outweigh the additional benefits, the further expansion of domestic agricultural production likely to result from British entry into the Common Market is even more open to criticism.

NOTES

1. Michael Butterwick and Edmund Neville Rolfe, Food, Farming and the Common Market (New York: Oxford University Press, 1968), p. 76.

2. Great Britain, Britain and the European Communities—An Economic Assessment, Cmnd. 4289 (London: HMSO, February, 1970).

3. FAO, Production Yearbook, 1969 (Rome, 1970), Table 3.

4. Great Britain, The United Kingdom and the European Communities, Cmnd. 4715 (London: HMSO, July, 1971), par. 93.

5. Ibid., par. 95.

6. FAO, Provisional Indicative Plan for World Agriculture (Rome, 1970).

7. The United Kingdom and the European Communities, par. 95.

8. See National Institute of Economic and Social Research, "The World Economy," Economic Review (London) (February, 1971), pp. 83-84 (section on commodity prices).

9. Great Britain, The National Plan, Cmnd. 2764 (London: HMSO, September, 1965), par. 25.

10. EDC for Agriculture, Agriculture's Import-Saving Role (London: National Economic Development Office, July, 1968).

11. Great Britain, Parliament, Parliamentary Debates (House of Commons), Vol. 773 (12 Nov., 1968), cols. 212-13.

12. Great Britain, Annual Review and Determination of Guarantees, Cmnd. 4321 (London: HMSO, 1970), par. 3.

13. Great Britain, Annual Review and Determination of Guarantees, Cmnd. 4623 (London: HMSO, 1971), pars. 2 and 7.

14. Ibid., pars. 5 and 6.

15. C. H. Blagburn, "Import Replacement by British Agriculture," Economic Journal, LX, 137 (March, 1950), 19-45; E. A. G. Robinson

and R. L. Marris, "The Use of Home Resources to Save Imports,"
Economic Journal, LX, 137 (March, 1950), 177-81; G. D. A. McDougall,
"The Use of Home Resources to Save Imports: A Comment," Economic
Journal, LX, 239 (September, 1950), 239, 629-31; E. A. G. Robinson and
R. L. Marris, "The Use of Home Resources to Save Imports: A Rejoin-
der," Economic Journal, LXI, 241 (March, 1951), 176-79; A. R. Bird,
"The Effect of Agricultural Price Support on the Balance of Payments
in the U.K.," Journal of Farm Economics, XXXIX, 5 (December, 1957),
1,714-23; E. A. G. Robinson, "The Cost of Agricultural Import-Saving,"
Three Banks Review, No. 40 (December, 1958), pp. 3-13; Gavin
McCrone, The Economics of Subsidising Agriculture (London: Allen
& Unwin, 1962), chap. v; and G. Ritson, "The Use of Home Resources
to Save Imports: A New Look," Journal of Agricultural Economics,
XXI, 1 (January, 1970), 121-29.

   16. Agriculture's Import-Saving Role, p. 33.

   17. Truman Phillips and Christopher Ritson, "Agricultural
Expansion and the UK Balance of Payments," National Westminister
Bank Quarterly Review (February, 1970), pp. 50-80.

   18. Ibid.

5

INTERNATIONAL
COMMODITY AGREEMENTS
AND GATT

In view of the significance to world food trade of U.K. entry into the EEC, the question arises about whether the effects cannot be regulated within the framework of worldwide commodity and trade agreements. Attempts to deal with agricultural problems through international action have, to date, mainly taken the form of establishing international commodity agreements or negotiations under GATT.

Although several international commodity agreements had their origin in the 1960's, they assumed importance in the Depression during the 1930's, when several attempts were made to raise the producer price of foodstuffs and raw materials by agreements between the governments of the producing countries. Tin, rubber, cotton, tea, coffee, cocoa, and wheat were among the products for which agreements were made. The usual pattern of these agreements was one of temporary success, leading to stimulation of production in countries outside the agreement, which, in turn, led to collapse.

The Havana Charter of 1944 proposed an International Trade Organization (ITO) that would include among its functions the formation and regulation of international commodity agreements. The ITO was never formed, however, and the main achievement resulting from the Havana Charter was GATT. During the closing years of World War II and the immediate postwar years, high hopes were entertained for the creation of a network of international commodity agreements, and, since 1945, many organizations—including the FAO, the U.N. Economic Commission for Latin America, the U.N. Economic and Social Council, and, since 1964, the United Nations Conference on Trade and Development (UNCTAD)—have been concerned with the promotion of international commodity agreements.

During this period, however, only five commodity agreements have been concluded—for wheat, sugar, coffee, tin, and olive oil. The olive oil agreement is not concerned with the regulation of international trade, and the effect of the International Wheat Agreement (IWA) on international trade has been intermittent and minor. The International Sugar Agreement does not cover the bulk of international trade in sugar and has had less effect than has the Commonwealth Sugar Agreement.

Probably the most effective of the postwar agreements has been the tin agreement, but, even in tin, there have been some severe falls in price, particularly in 1958 (partly due to an increase in tin exports from the Soviet bloc countries, which later were brought within the agreement), and there have also been some sharp rises in tin prices, which the agreement was unable to prevent. (Tin is ideally suited for regulation by means of a buffer stock, since it is stable and homogeneous and since the quantity used annually is small.)

In its 1963 world economic survey, the United Nations commented on the lack of success of international commodity agreements and pointed to the importance of certain aspects of organization and operation.[1] These include the comprehensiveness of coverage, the realism of the price range to be defended, the capacity to finance and handle stocks, and the willingness of participants to make periodic adjustments in rights and obligations to keep them in line with external developments.

Two main practical difficulties have been encountered. First, as previously mentioned, raising the producer price above the level that would otherwise have prevailed will stimulate production outside the countries participating in the agreement, as well as in low-cost producing countries and in consuming countries within the agreement, and will also stimulate the search for substitutes. Most temperate-zone foodstuffs can be grown in most countries of the world, and, if, for example, an attempt were made to raise the price of wheat in the world market by means of production and export quotas imposed by the major exporting countries, production elsewhere would rise.

Producers of tropical products—such as coffee, tea, and cocoa—are in a stronger position, but, even with these, the number of countries that can expand or enter production is larger than appears at first sight. The primary product that most closely approximates a monopoly situation is tin, which is exported on a large scale by only six countries (Indonesia, Malaya, Thailand, Bolivia, Congo, Kinshasa and Nigeria), but high tin prices in the early 1950's gave an impetus to methods of production that economized in the use of tin and also stimulated the search for substitutes.

For these reasons, the power of the producers of any commodity to maintain agreements on prices is very limited. If a major consuming country or group of countries, however, wishes to initiate a price-raising agreement, there is no reason to suppose that it cannot do so, since producing countries have few alternative outlets. There is no obvious reason why consuming countries should take this step, but, with the possibility of British entry into the Common Market, it has become a serious possibility.

Great Britain is by far the largest importer of many temperate-zone agricultural products (in many cases, the only large importer), and Great Britain and the six EEC nations combined would exercise a dominant influence on world trade in most agricultural products, far outweighing the other two major industrial areas—the United States and Japan—in importance as importers. (See Table 26.)

The second practical difficulty that has been encountered in international commodity agreements is that, when the price of a particular product rises or falls, there is no way of knowing whether this is a temporary change that can be smoothed out (for example, by buffer stock operations) or whether it presages a long-term change in demand or supply conditions to which the stabilizing authority should adapt. This problem can be dealt with if the stabilizing body adopts a system of basing its prices in any period on the average of prices in the preceding period (as in the proposed "crawling peg" system for foreign exchange rates).

The aims of international commodity agreements are usually stated to be the stabilization of prices to producers and/or the elimination of undesirable or excessive price fluctuations, prices that are reasonable to producers and consumers, and the stabilization of producers' incomes. These criteria give little guidance in any practical situation, and the objectives of price and income stabilization may conflict. For example, a large crop will usually result in lower prices but may not result in lower incomes for producers unless markets are limited and the elasticity of demand is low. There is an even more basic difficulty, the problem of efficiency, which is mentioned later in this chapter.

THE BAUMGARTNER-PISANI PLAN

Since the start of the negotiations between Great Britain and the Common Market countries in 1961, several proposals have been put forward for international commodity agreements as a means of solving the agricultural problems and of trying to harmonize the EEC's agricultural policy with those of third countries. In a White Paper of August, 1962, the British negotiator, Mr. Heath, said that all the governments concerned, including the British Government, had agreed to promote "world-wide agreements for the principal agricultural products," which would cover, among other things, "the price and production policy to be followed by the exporting and importing countries, the minimum and maximum quantities to enter international trade, and the special aspects of trade with developing countries."[2]

In the same month, it was announced that the Common Market countries and the applicant countries would call an international conference to agree upon the principles of arrangements for grains, meat, dairy products, and sugar. The task of the conference would be to find a reasonable compromise between the interests of the importing and the exporting countries and to ensure the rational development of international trade.

The best known of the proposals for international commodity agreements, which had the support of the EEC Commission, was the Baumgartner-Pisani Plan, put forward in November, 1961, by Mr. Baumgartner, then French minister of finance, at a meeting of GATT, and Mr. Pisani, then French minister of agriculture, to the FAO. The plan aimed at raising the c.i.f. price of imported food in the importing countries to that of the producer price of domestically produced food in the importing countries. It was initially for wheat but was intended to apply to all grains and, in principle, to all foodstuffs.

It was recognized that the increase in world prices might lead to an increase in production in the exporting countries and elsewhere and that it would therefore be necessary to reach an understanding about production and marketing policies, with agreed-upon production quotas, planned exports, and common stockpiling policies. Any surplus above the amount for domestic consumption and regular commercial exports would then be disposed of by special noncommercial sales on a coordinated basis to underdeveloped countries.

Although the outcome would depend on the final price level in the enlarged EEC and on the production and market shares agreed upon, the Baumgartner-Pisani proposals would have added greatly to the import bill of the importing countries (especially Great Britain) and would have come up against the practical difficulties of production control of temperate-zone foodstuffs.

It was based on the assumption that the prevailing price of foodstuffs, especially wheat, on the world market was artificially low as a result of subsidized exports, at that time an assumption that might have had some basis in fact regarding grains, due to the U.S. surplus disposal program. This later diminished, however, with the run-down of the U.S. grain stockpile and more effective production control there.

In the late 1960's and the early 1970's, dumping and subsidization in world markets was largely in dairy products and, to a considerable extent, a direct or indirect result of the EEC agricultural policy, which makes explicit provision for subsidies on exports to third countries. Dumped exports have always been quantitatively minor in relation to the volume of world trade in any product, and low export prices of New Zealand dairy products are the result not of dumping but of low production costs.

As far as the importing countries and their domestic farmers are concerned, the problems arising from dumping are not difficult to deal with, since both the existence and the degree of dumping are easy to determine. It is usually easy to find out domestic consumer prices in the exporting country—even when that country is, for example, Poland, Czechoslovakia, or Yugoslavia—and export prices can always be determined by taking the value and volume figures of exports from published foreign trade statistics. The c.i.f. import price will, of course, also be known. A difference between domestic and export prices in the exporting country substantially larger than can be accounted for by consumption taxes and distribution costs indicates dumping.

Provision for antidumping duties is made in GATT (Article VI). The British antidumping act of 1956, the Customs Duties (Dumping and Subsidies) Act, provides not only that the existence of dumping must be proved, but also that "material injury" must be caused or threatened to home producers before antidumping duties are imposed, and it has been criticized by domestic producers on the grounds that it is too slow to take effect. The main points—the minor importance of dumping on world prices and the ease with which its existence can be determined—remain, however.

The alleged justification provided by dumping for international commodity agreements tended to drop into the background in later discussions, but, in the July, 1971, British Government White Paper, it is still being argued that international commodity agreements will help to solve the problems arising from British entry into the EEC.[3]

In the context of a discussion of New Zealand dairy products and lamb, it is stated that

> among the considerations of which account will be taken during this review [of New Zealand's position, to be under-taken during the third year after Great Britain's accession to the EEC] will be the progress made towards an effective world agreement on milk products and the question of New Zealand's progress towards diversification of its economy and its exports. The Community has undertaken to make every effort to promote the conclusion of an international agreement on dairy products; and to pursue a policy which will not frustrate New Zealand's efforts to diversify. This should help New Zealand to increase her earnings in other markets.[4]

From this it appears that, inside the enlarged EEC, Great Britain will try to reduce the effect of subsidized EEC dairy exports on New Zealand's dairy exports and will press for increased access for New Zealand products, other than dairy products, to the enlarged EEC and for all New Zealand exports to markets other than the EEC. Although these efforts may help New Zealand, they will be of much less benefit from the wider economic standpoint than would a direct attack on the level of protection for dairy products within the en-larged EEC and in other countries. In general, the aim of promoting international commodity agreements is meaningless unless the content of the agreement is specified.

GATT'S APPROACH

The main forum for dealing with barriers to international trade, in agricultural as well as industrial goods, is, of course, GATT, established in 1947, which has now held six rounds of tariff conferences—Geneva, 1947; Annecy, 1949; Torquay, 1951; Geneva, 1956; the Dillion Round, 1960-61; and the Kennedy Round, 1964-67. The most significant of these was the Kennedy Round, which aimed at, and to a large extent achieved, a 50 per cent reduction in the tariffs on industrial goods (other than in underdeveloped or primary producing countries) that existed when the round began.

Before the Kennedy Round, GATT negotiations had been on an item-by-item and country-by-country basis. In the Kennedy Round, the participating countries adopted the procedure of linear across-the-board reduction of all tariffs, with lists of exceptions; these latter became such an important point of the bargaining that the "linear" concept became somewhat blurred, and the round became more like the previous item-by-item negotiations.

The cumulative result of the GATT rounds, however, has now been to reduce tariffs on most products imported into major industrial countries to minor dimensions compared with their prewar and immediate postwar levels. "These six rounds of tariff negotiations [from the Geneva Round in 1947 to the Kennedy Round in 1964-67] have resulted in the reduction of world tariff levels to a degree that would probably have surprised the most sanguine proponents of the I T.O."[5] The average tariff on dutiable imports into the United States, fell from 47 per cent in 1934 to 12 per cent in 1955 and will fall to just under 8 per cent after the implementation of the Kennedy Round tariff cuts in 1973.[6]

Although there is nothing in the constitution of GATT that excludes agricultural products and although the general and total prohibition on quantitative restrictions on imports applies equally to agriculture (with the exception of a proviso in Article XI 2 (c), which allows quantitative restrictions on imports if needed to implement government policies restricting domestic production of the same product), progress on reducing obstacles to international trade in agricultural products under GATT has been negligible.

Indeed, since 1947, there has fairly certainly been an increase in the degree of agricultural protection in many countries, including probably the major importing countries—Great Britain, the United States, and West Germany—that has been reflected in their higher degree of self-sufficiency in many agricultural products (although technical progress has also been a factor).

It would be difficult to conclude that the GATT's record in the sphere of temperate agricultural products is other than one of failure. Not only is effective protection in all likelihood higher on average than in any other sector of the economy, but there are many indications that the rate of effective protection is increasing.[7]

The basic principle that underlies negotiations in GATT is, as its Preamble states, that negotiations are to be "on a reciprocal and mutually advantageous" basis. Apart from any other consideration, unilateral reduction of tariffs or nontariff barriers by one country alone would probably lead to balance-of-payments difficulties for the country concerned, while, if reductions are multilateral, it is probable that exports as well as imports will increase.

In practice, the principle of reciprocity has been taken to mean the volume of imports to which the tariff concession applied. Exemptions to this principle have been made regarding the underdeveloped countries, which have not been compelled to make tariff cuts corresponding to those that have applied to their exports, and regarding the primary producing countries. Both of these groups have raised some of their tariffs on "infant industry" grounds.

As long as there is no prospect of expanding their agricultural exports, the temperate-zone agricultural exporting countries have little alternative but to maintain high industrial tariffs. As Eric Wyndham White, formerly director-general of GATT, has said,

> The basis of the General Agreement is that the parties
> believe in international specialisation and exchange, and
> believe in the various areas and countries of the world
> specialising in the things that they are best fitted to pro-
> duce. It is not a doctrine which can be applied in one
> field and excluded in another.[8]

During the Kennedy Round of negotiations, Canada, Australia, New Zealand, and the Union of South Africa obtained some degree of exemption from the linear tariff cuts on the grounds that they would not be able to obtain reciprocity regarding their agricultural exports.

Before the Kennedy Round, the United States made it a condition of participation that agriculture should be included in the negotiations. Hence, agricultural problems were considered to a much greater extent than was the case in previous GATT negotiations, with the objective of concluding international commodity agreements and also of agreements on "reasonable access" for exporting countries based on degrees of self-sufficiency in the importing countries.

The second of these two objectives, however, had to be abandoned, due to the difficulty of getting agreement on what constituted reasonable access and because agreement on this would, in effect, involve a concession by the importing countries regarding their freedom to fix domestic producer price levels. The main outcome of the Kennedy Round, regarding agriculture, was the International Grains Arrangement.

This involved two main features. The first was basically the incorporation of the IWA, which had been in existence since 1949. The IWA had permitted a wide range of price fluctuation (162.5-202.5 U.S. cents per bushel for the indicator grade of Manitoba No.1 wheat, under a 1962 agreement, that was continued unchanged until its

replacement by the International Grains Arrangement in July, 1967).
Except for the years 1949-53, when prices for nonagreement sales of
wheat were above the upper limit, world market prices had stayed
within the IWA range.

Under the International Grains Arrangement, it was at first at-
tempted to obtain a fairly large increase in maximum and minimum
prices. This was opposed by the main importing countries—Great
Britain and Japan. In any event, some increase in prices was attained,
on the assumption that a shortage of wheat was likely, but this expec-
tation has turned out to be unjustified, and, in 1968-69 a number of
sales were made at prices below the new minimum.

The second feature of the International Grains Arrangement,
which was not part of the IWA was an agreement on food aid, in which
the participating countries agreed to provide 4.5 million tons of grain
per year (in wheat, coarse grains, or the cash equivalent) as food aid;
42 per cent of this was to be provided by the United States and 23 per
cent by the EEC.[9] The International Grains Arrangement took effect
on July 1, 1968, for a period of three years.

A number of reductions were made in agricultural tariffs, but
these are of very minor importance in restricting international trade
in agriculture, compared with levies, quotas, and internal price support
and subsidy arrangements. Thus, the temperate-zone agricultural
exporting countries gained little from the Kennedy Round as far as
their exports were concerned. It is likely, however, that agriculture
will play a vital part in future GATT negotiations.

For this reason, it is essential to try to estimate the degree of
agricultural protection both for individual products and for agriculture
as a whole, so that pressure can be put on the countries with the highest
degree of agricultural protection to make the largest reductions (possibly in percentage as well as absolute terms), as tends to happen in GATT
negotiations on industrial tariffs despite the adoption, in principle, of
the linear reduction method (which implies equal percentage cuts for
all countries) in the Kennedy Round. The question of measuring the
degree of agricultural protection will be returned to in Chapter 6.

THE PROBLEM OF EFFICIENCY

The problem of efficiency is also the heart of the problem of
international commodity agreements. The essential feature of a
commodity agreement, if it is to operate to the benefit both of

producers and consumers, is a provision for a periodical reallocation of the production or export shares of the participating countries in order to expand the share of the low-cost producers. Such a provision is implicit in the constitution and objectives of the postwar commodity agreements (which, unlike the prewar ones, have equal representation of consumers and producers). For example, the objectives of the International Tin Agreement are stated as follows:

(a) To prevent or alleviate widespread unemployment or under-employment and other serious difficulties which are likely to result from maladjustment between the supply of and demand for tin; (b) to prevent excessive fluctuations in the price of tin and to obtain a reasonable degree of stability of price on a basis which will secure long-term equilibrium between supply and demand; (c) to secure adequate supplies of tin at reasonable prices at all times; and (d) to provide a framework for the consideration and development of measures to promote the progressively more economic production of tin while protecting tin deposits from unnecessary waste or premature abandonment. [Emphasis added.][10]

Some of the wider proposals for regulating international commodity trade have also included a proposal to this effect. In 1955, a Special Agreement on Commodity Agreements was proposed, to exist side by side with GATT, which, in addition to the aims of "a reasonable degree of stability on the basis of prices that are fair to consumers and provide a reasonable return to producers," "preventing shortages in world supplies or the burdensome accumulation of stocks," also aimed "direct production to places where world market demand can be satisfied in the most effective and economic manner."

The proposal for a Special Agreement never became operative, however, and none of the proposed or existing commodity agreements has recognized explicitly that satisfying requirements in the most economic manner involves—if there is any form of production or export control—a periodical reallocation of market shares in order to increase the share of the low-cost producers. In other words, the agreements have been unwilling to recognize explicitly that there are large differences in efficiency between producing countries. Once this fact is recognized, such phrases as "prices reasonable to producers" or prices that provide producers with a "reasonable return" can be seen to be meaningless.

If the proposal for reallocating production shares in an international commodity agreement in favor of the more efficient producers were adopted, it would obviously be essential to have a generally agreed-upon measure of (national) efficiency in the production of the commodity concerned. For this purpose, the proposal put forward in Chapter 6 for using producer prices as a criterion of efficiency could be used. Since producer prices also provide the best possible indication of the degree of protection that agricultural commodities in any country receive, commodity agreements could be linked with a gradual, planned, and worldwide dismantling of agricultural protectionism.

One problem that would arise if Great Britain entered the Common Market would be that, in the enlarged EEC, after the end of the transition period, there would be a uniform producer price level (after allowing for transport costs and other noncompetition-distorting variations). In this situation, either the EEC would have to be treated as a single producer country in any international commodity agreement or some criterion of efficiency other than producer prices— presumably costs, profits, or value-added—would have to be used.

In the first eventuality—and, indeed, even if one disregards the question of international commodity agreements—it is to be hoped that, within the enlarged EEC, there would operate some system of gradually raising the share of the internal market held by the low-cost producing countries. Although an expansion of production in these countries (mainly Denmark, Great Britain, and Ireland for temperate-zone products) might, in any case, be expected to lead to higher marginal costs, there would be a danger, if no such explicit linking of efficiency and market share existed—not only that consumers and efficiency in the allocation of resources would suffer, but also that agricultural efficiency in the low-cost producer countries would decline and their producer prices would rise, as competitive pressure on them to keep down their costs diminished.

A SIDE ISSUE: THE UNDERDEVELOPED COUNTRIES

This book is concerned with temperate-zone agriculture, and the problems of agricultural producers in underdeveloped countries are not pursued. It may be noted, however, that most of the points made about commodity agreements here apply equally to commodity agreements intended to benefit producers in underdeveloped countries. Unless a criterion exists for reallocating production shares in favor of low-cost producers, such agreements are merely devices to try to raise prices.

There are many commodities whose prices can be raised in the short run without adverse repercussions on the producers, but, in the long run, higher prices are very likely to stimulate both the search for substitutes and production outside the agreement; in other words, the long-run price elasticities of supply and demand are usually much higher than those in the short run.

It has also been argued that commodity agreements may harm the producing country by dissuading it from shifting resources from products for which demand has fallen to more profitable lines of production.[11] One of the aims of UNCTAD when it was established in 1964 was to promote commodity agreements, but this aim now appears to have fallen into the background.

The Final Act of the 1964 conference (which set up UNCTAD as a permanent body) enumerated two groups of provisions that it considered necessary to increase the export earnings of developing countries: (1) provisions for international commodity arrangements, with the object of stimulating a dynamic and steady growth and ensuring reasonable predictability in the real export earnings of the developing countries; and (2) provision for a program of measures and actions for the removal of obstacles and discriminatory practices and for an expansion of market opportunities for primary commodity exports and for an increase in consumption and imports of primary products in developed countries.[12] (The second objective is, of course, a very valid and important one.)

Food aid to underdeveloped countries has long been supported by agricultural producers' organizations in the developed countries and has been advocated by the IFAP since 1959. For the first time in an international commodity agreement, it was adopted as part of the International Grains Arrangement in 1967. In the late 1950's and the early 1960's, the main donor of food surpluses to underdeveloped countries was the United States, which had accumulated large stocks of many foodstuffs, especially grains.

In recent years, U.S. disposals have become less important, partly as a result of more effective production control in the United States and the consequent run-down of the stocks held there by the Commodity Credit Corporation, and the EEC has emerged as an important donor. In the three years 1968-71, the EEC was responsible for about one-quarter of all food aid.[13]

The question of food aid is too wide to be pursued here. It is generally recognized that it is only a temporary solution, the long-term goal being the increase of domestic food production in the underdeveloped countries, and that food aid may have a harmful effect on these domestic producers, as well as on low-cost commercial suppliers of food to the underdeveloped countries. Conversely, it may be that food aid constitutes a net addition to total aid to underdeveloped countries, which would be lower if food aid did not exist.

If this aspect of international commodity agreements is further developed, it is to be hoped—for the benefit of the receiving countries, as well as for others—that the aid will be through multilaterally financed purchases of food from low-cost producing countries, rather than tied to purchases from countries that happen to have disposable surpluses. Not only does the latter solution reduce the incentive to the surplus countries to tackle their surplus problem by reducing producer prices, but a given sum of money devoted, for example, to sending dairy products to underdeveloped countries will be of much greater value to the recipient countries if used to purchase dairy products from Denmark or New Zealand rather than from Great Britain, the United States, or the Common Market countries.

NOTES

1. United Nations, World Economic Survey, Vol. 1: Trade and Development: Trends, Needs and Policies (Geneva, 1965).

2. Great Britain, The United Kingdom and the European Community: Report by the Lord Privy Seal on the Meeting with Ministers of Member States of the European Economic Community at Brussels from August 1-5, Cmnd. 1805 (London: HMSO, August, 1962), par. 15.

3. Great Britain, The United Kingdom and the European Communities, Cmnd. 4715 (London: HMSO, July, 1971).

4. Ibid., par. 107.

5. K. W. Dam, The G.A.T.T.: Law and International Economic Organization (Chicago: University of Chicago Press, 1970), p. 56.

6. H. S. Piquet, Statement to the Committee on Ways and Means, U.S. House of Representatives, Second Session on Tariff and Trade Proposals, Part 10, June 5, 1970 (Washington: U.S. Government Printing Office, 1970), p. 2681.

7. K. W. Dam, op.cit., p. 257.

8. Eric Wyndham White, The Activities of the GATT, address given at the Graduate Institute for International Studies, Geneva, December, 1956 (Geneva: GATT, 1957). 1956, p. 14.

9. CEC, "Grain Crops" (London: Commonwealth Secretariat, 1969), p. 162.

10. International Tin Agreement, London, March 1, 1954, Cmnd. 12 (London: HMSO, 1956).

11. This argument is developed by Sir Sydney Caine, Prices for Primary Producers (London: Institute of Economic Affairs, 1964).

12. K. M. Hagras, United Nations Conference on Trade and Development (New York: Praeger, 1965).

13. John Lambert, "Food Aid—the EEC's Record," European Community (November, 1970).

6

**EFFICIENCY
IN AGRICULTURE**

CONCEPTS AND MEASUREMENT

The idea of efficiency, like the partly interchangeable one of productivity, is one of the most widely used in economics but, nevertheless, raises serious problems of definition and measurement. In economic theory, efficiency is widely used to mean the allocation of given productive resources, using fixed techniques of production, to satisfy given consumers' preferences. Thus, one book states that "economic efficiency was assured when prices were equal to production costs and costs were computed from the marginal productivities of the factors of production."[1]

In practice, however, economic efficiency is not merely a matter of allocating resources between different uses and combining factors of production in such a manner as to equalize their price and their marginal productivity, but of devising techniques of production that reduce costs. The latter point is recognized in the following definition of economic efficiency from a dictionary of economic terms:

> The efficiency with which scarce resources are used and organized to achieve stipulated economic ends. In competitive conditions, the lower the cost per unit of output, without sacrifice of quality, in relation to the value or price of the finished article, the greater the economic efficiency of the productive organization.[2]

Discussion of definitions is usually both tedious and fruitless, but there are two major ambiguities in the concept of efficiency that must be cleared up before any practical problem is tackled. The first

is the confusion between economic and technical efficiency. Using the
most up-to-date methods and the most advanced techniques is not
always economically rational, since it may not necessarily result in
lower costs per unit of output and/or demand conditions may not be
such as to absorb the increased output at the cost at which it is produced. Anyone familiar with basic economics is unlikely to fall into
this confusion.

A second ambiguity, however, is prevalent both among economists
and the general public. This is the failure to distinguish between
"partial" and "total" measures of productivity. Generally, the term
"productivity," used without qualification, means the productivity of
labor. The difficulty here arises because the productivity of labor
can usually be raised by combining a fixed quantity of labor with a
larger quantity of capital (or, in agriculture, of land), as well as by
better management and technical innovation.

A recent study in Great Britain claimed that the nationalized
industries were more efficient than the private sector was, because
output per man in the nationalized sector had been increasing more
rapidly.[3] This overlooks two important factors: the large capital
investment programs of the nationalized industries and their generally
higher degree of monopoly power (that is, lower elasticity of demand)
than exists in most private industries.

That labor productivity can usually be raised by combining a
fixed quantity of labor with a larger quantity of capital also sometimes
leads to confusion in regard to productivity agreements, when it may
be overlooked that only a small part of the historical rise in labor
productivity is due directly to action by labor.

Nor can the main problem of measurement be overcome by taking
output per unit of capital in conjunction with output per unit of labor.
It will often be found, at least in the short run, that labor productivity
will vary inversely with capital productivity, and many changes in
productivity—resulting, for example, from economies of scale, technical progress, and managerial improvement—cannot be attributed
accurately either to capital or to labor.

In comparing countries, it is usually safe to assume that income
per head is a good indication of the efficiency of the whole economy
and that countries can be arranged in order of efficiency corresponding
to their per capita incomes, with the United States at the top of the
scale, Western Europe further down, and the underdeveloped countries
at the bottom.

Incomes cannot, however, be taken as an indication of efficiency in comparing different industries within a country or in comparing the same industry in different countries.[4] This is mainly because, in most economies, wage increases in one industry tend to be generalized throughout the economy sooner or later by the operation of the "comparability" principle, as well as by effects on the supply of labor in competing industries and organizations. There are several other, less important difficulties, including different degrees of monopoly in both the product and the labor markets.

Labor productivity is of vital importance in determining a country's standard of living—indeed, it is the standard of living—but it cannot be assumed that anything that raises labor productivity in one industry, or even in the economy as a whole, is desirable. Other factors of production are also in short supply. Whether it is desirable to raise labor productivity in one industry or firm depends, among other things, on the supply—and the cost—of additional capital compared with the expected increase in output and the price at which that output can be sold.

An increase in labor productivity can, in general, be used only to show an increase in total efficiency if no other changes have taken place, and, although this may sometimes happen in comparing the situation at two different times in one country, it is almost impossible to envisage a situation in international comparisons in which labor productivity measures can yield significant results. The agricultural economist H. Jorring has written:

> The term "productivity measure" implies that productivity can be measured by partial ratios. Because I think that this is mostly not the case I prefer to avoid the term productivity in connection with single input ratios and use a more neutral term, viz. ratio.

> The significance of the partial productivity measure depends on whether it may be assumed that the ceteris paribus clause is approximately satisfied with respect to the excluded input, or whether the excluded input is quantitatively so unimportant that a change in the volume of it has in any case no great influence.

> In most cases these conditions are not satisfied. A striking example is the use of changes in production per head of animals, e.g. litre of milk per cow or number of eggs per hen as productivity measures. It is not even clear to

which input the output is related in this case, but certainly
most of the input is excluded. Such figures may be important for certain purposes, and possibly may even serve to
explain in part differences in productivity, but they have
no meaning as measures of productivity per se. Most of
these kinds of relationships have only a technical significance and it is only exceptionally that a wider economic
significance can be assigned to them.[5]

Apart from partial (and usually misleading) measures of output
per man, per unit of capital, or per unit of land, the most widely used
measure of the efficiency of an individual firm is to take profits
(usually expressed as a percentage of capital employed, or sometimes
per unit of sales). Although this is, in many ways, the most useful
criterion and measure of efficiency available, it is subject to two
difficulties (particularly in manufacturing). A firm that is in a
monopolistic position can raise its profits by raising its price; and
(particularly with consumer goods) consumer ignorance of quality
may have the same result.

In comparing two firms in the same industry, however, if both
are producing a product that is the same regarding both objective and
subjective quality, then profits are probably the best single measure
of efficiency. But profitability cannot be used in comparing the
efficiency of one industry with that of another, since their demand and
cost conditions will be different.

Profitability might be used to compare the efficiency of the
same industry in two different countries (provided tariffs are not
markedly different and there is no other form of government intervention), but it is of little use in comparing the efficiency of agriculture in two different countries, due to the high degree of government
intervention in all countries, especially in temperate-zone agriculture.

One way of clarifying the issue is to ask why one should measure
productivity or efficiency. Most studies on the subject have been done
for one of two reasons. The first—the approach of the fundamental
researcher—is to try to disentangle the reasons why productivity
varies between countries (in one industry or the whole economy) and
why productivity has changed over time (in one industry or country).[6]
The ultimate aim of this kind of research is to try to discover and
to quantify the causes of economic progress.* The second approach—

---

*It is desirable, for example, to be able to say that the increase

that of the management consultant or productivity adviser—consists
of comparing individual firms, and occasionally industries, with the
object of enabling the more backward firms to raise their economic
performance to the level of the better ones.

The first type of investigation, apart from its value as scientific
or historical knowledge, has the ultimate "operational" aim of enabling
governments to see what should be done to raise their rate of economic
growth—should they devote effort primarily (and, more important, to
what extent) to raising capital investment, improving education, promoting technological development, or some other course of action?
The second approach aims to guide managers on how to improve their
firm's performance. The goal of this book is different from both of
these.

EFFICIENCY AND AGRICULTURAL POLICY

The aim of this volume is neither to ascertain the reasons why
efficiency in agriculture varies between countries or changes over
time, nor to find out how efficiency in a particular branch of agriculture, on individual farms, or with regard to agriculture as a whole
can be increased. Little research has, in fact, been done on the first
question, in comparison with the fairly extensive work on efficiency
in manufacturing. The second has been the subject of a good deal of
study, which forms the basis of the work of the National Agricultural
Advisory Service in Great Britain and similar organizations in other
countries. Of concern here is the existence—and, as far as possible,
the measurement—of differences in agricultural productivity between
countries and the implications of this for national economic policy.

The bearing on national policy is primarily that which is raised
in all discussions of international trade policy—that is, the benefits
to consumers and to economic efficiency (through using resources of
labor and capital in the line of production in any country in which they
are most efficient or least inefficient) that result from free trade.
The question is considerably more important in agriculture than in
manufacturing or in the service sector, however, in view of the much
greater degree of protection and intervention that all governments

---

in output per head between 1900 and 1970 was due in x per cent to
more capital, y per cent to technical change, z per cent to better
education, and so on with the other factors involved.

practice in the agricultural sphere. Criteria for agricultural policy—
the degree of protection to be adopted for agriculture as a whole, the
allocation between products, the degree of self-sufficiency to be aimed
at, and the cost of these policies—are seldom made explicit and, indeed, generally do not exist (although some economists might argue
that they can be inferred from government behavior).

The concept of free trade or free imports, however, is also much
more complex in agriculture than in industry, owing to the universality
of government intervention. It cannot always be assumed that the price
on the world market or import prices for any country represent the
result of a free interplay of supply and demand, because of the existence
of dumping (that is, export subsidization). When one country engages
in dumping, the export price of other producing countries may be
forced down, and, for some products, it can hardly be said that there
is a free world market at all.

The existence of dumping can also be overestimated, however.
It is frequently argued, for example, in connection with the probable
rise of domestic consumer prices for butter in Great Britain if it
joined the Common Market that the present consumer price of butter
is artifically low and is the result of dumping. This is true of many
butter-exporting countries but is not true of the most important ones—
New Zealand or Denmark—whose butter export prices are the result
of low production costs—that is, high efficiency.

It is, therefore, of considerable importance to national policy
to try to arrive at a clear understanding of the precise degree of
difference in agricultural efficiency between countries. A government
intervening in its domestic agriculture should be aware of how different sectors of its own agriculture, and its agriculture as a whole,
compare with other countries if it is to apportion a given degree of
protection with a minimum economic loss. It goes without saying
that it should also be clear about its reasons for protecting agriculture—social, regional, balance of payments, or some other—although
frequently governments are not.

Also, if international negotiations for the reduction of agricultural protection are ever to make any real headway—as pointed
out earlier, progress in reducing agricultural protection has been
very small in the postwar period compared with that in reducing
tariffs and other import restrictions on manufactured goods—then it
is essential to have an idea of the degree of protection that different
countries have at the start of the negotiations.

For Great Britain, there is a more pressing reason at present that differences in agricultural efficiency, costs, and prices between countries should be closely examined. This is the prospect of entry into the Common Market. In addition to the potentially serious effect on the balance-of-payments and the cost-of-living, there would be a major shift in the volume and composition of agricultural production in Great Britain and the other applicant countries (and, to a lesser extent, in the six EEC nations) as a result of substantial—indeed, unprecedented—shifts in producer prices.

Both the prices themselves and the probable effect of price changes on production are major issues in the negotiations, and a number of attempts have been made to estimate the effect of the probable changes if Great Britain enters, but, in these estimates, the question of efficiency has tended to fade into the background.

THE MEASUREMENT OF AGRICULTURAL EFFICIENCY

It would be possible to approach the problem of measuring agricultural efficiency by taking the main factors of production—land, labor, and capital—and the ratio of each to total output, and then trying to arrive at a composite figure of inputs. The problem here, again, is that increasing the quantity of one factor while holding the quantity of other factors constant will usually (as the textbook law of diminishing returns states) result in a lower marginal productivity in the factor whose quantity is increased.

Disregarding marginal productivity and turning, instead, to the more relevant and easily measurable average productivity, one will usually find in making international comparisons that the productivity of the two most easily measurable factors of production—labor and land—is related more to the total supply of one of these factors in relation to the supply of the other than to the effectiveness with which it is used.

Agricultural output per unit of land area is very high in the United Arab Republic, the Netherlands, Taiwan, and Japan, which have a high population density. Output per unit of land is low and output per man is high in such countries as Canada, Australia, Argentina, and Uruguay, which have a plentiful supply of land and a low population density.[7]

In such a league table, there can be no implication that the countries with a high agricultural output per unit of land area are more efficient than those with a low output. The relative position is merely the result of the factor endowments of the countries concerned. Conversely, output per person employed in agriculture is extremely high in New Zealand, Australia, the United States, and Canada, reflecting mainly the large area of land worked by each person employed and, to a lesser extent, the large capital input.

For these reasons, it is not proposed here to work with figures of output per man or per hectare in comparing agricultural efficiency between countries. Some of the other problems that arise in comparing efficiency by means of these figures may be mentioned, however, for the light they throw on the question of efficiency and its measurement.

Where labor is concerned, it is desirable to take total man-hours worked rather than number of persons employed, in view of the large number of part-time workers in agriculture in many countries and since, in many countries, full-time workers in agriculture are not fully occupied throughout the year (although, on the latter point, it could be argued that keeping workers fully occupied is one of the most important aspects of efficiency and, hence, that output per worker is, in this respect, an indication of the efficiency of agriculture).

Figures of man-hours worked are much more difficult to obtain than census figures of numbers of persons employed in agriculture. Regarding part-time labor—farmers' wives and children—it is necessary to make some arbitrary assumption, for example, that a part-time worker should count as half a full-time worker. But, in addition, many small farmers have some outside occupation, and this is usually disregarded in calculations of farmers' output and income.

Turning to land, obviously it is agricultural land rather than total land area that is relevant. Figures of agricultural land are available for most countries. Measuring the input or stock of capital is difficult in manufacturing and much more so in agriculture, where much of the capital stock is made up of the results of possibly unpaid labor of the farmer, such as drainage, hedges, farm buildings, and so on.

The inadequacy of limited physical measures—such as crop yield per acre, milk yield per cow, or eggs produced per year per hen—as an indication of efficiency has already been noted. Taken together with other statistics and information, however, these figures are useful for many purposes, particularly in trying to increase the efficiency of backward farms, sectors of agriculture, or countries.

For example, rice yields per hectare are three or four times as large in Japan as in other rice-producing countries of Asia—Burma, Thailand, India, Pakistan, and Indonesia—despite similar soil and climate conditions. This fact indicates the extent to which rice yields in the latter could be raised, given more capital and (even more important) more skilful and intensive labor, the adoption of higher-yielding strains of rice, better marketing and transport arrangements, and so on.

The physical yield of any one product or group of products, however, is only a limited indicator of efficiency, whatever the purpose for which efficiency is being measured. As the FAO has pointed out,

> More significant than either crop yields or livestock yields by themselves is the over-all productivity of land, the whole output from each hectare of land used for agriculture. For while the individual yields reflect the efficiency of crop husbandry or livestock husbandry, the over-all productivity also takes into account the managerial skill with which the various farm enterprises are integrated to increase the total farm output. Suitable rotations, for example, can obviate the need for fallow, typical of many less developed agricultures. Catch crops can be sown to utilise moisture or fertility remaining after the main crop has been harvested. Mixed farming with crops and livestock gives the opportunity of conserving fodder from the flush season for use in lean periods, of using for animal feed the crop residues which might otherwise be wasted, and at the same time of improving the fertility of the soil. The over-all productivity also reflects the opportunities to produce high-value crops, e.g. tobacco, or in suitable climates or under irrigation to raise more than one crop per year from the same land.[8]

The most usual and possibly the most useful measure of efficiency in manufacturing and the service trades—the profitability of the individual producer unit—is less reliable in agriculture, because, in all countries, the profitability of agriculture as a whole and of its component parts is largely the result of government decisions. Profitability is, of course, of great value in comparing farms or sectors of agriculture within a particular country, but it is of little or no use in making international comparisons.

Production per unit of land, labor, or capital as a measure of productive efficiency is subject to the same difficulties in measuring inputs as it is in manufacturing, as well as some additional problems. The output may be easier to measure, since it is more homogeneous, but, because of the large variations in the ratio of land to labor between countries, the figures of land and labor productivity are, to a large extent, a reflection of these different factor endowments rather than of efficiency. Detailed physical measures—yields per cow, per acre, per hen—are even less helpful, except as a starting point for further investigations.

It may, however, be possible to short-circuit these difficulties and work with a measure of efficiency that is relevant to national policy-making, although not to explaining productivity differences or to productivity "missionary" work. This measure is obtained simply by comparing producer prices for particular products in different countries. This is easiest in the case of cereals, which are homogeneous in quality and where international differences in efficiency are probably larger than these in meat and dairy products. The price paid per bushel to producers for wheat, in 1970-71, was $1.29 in Argentina, $1.47 in Canada, $1.65 in Australia, $2.00 in the United States, $2.01 in Great Britain, $2.28 in France, and $2.58 in West Germany.[9]

It may be inferred that this scale also represents the efficiency of wheat producers in these countries. Whatever the reason—climate and soil, historical factors, managerial efficiency—farmers in Australia, Canada, and Argentina can produce wheat at much lower prices than can farmers in Europe. In fact, the most important reason for the greater efficiency of Australian and Canadian cereal producers is the larger average size of farm, itself a result of the availability of land and the absence of population pressure such as affected agricultural areas in Europe before the twentieth century. Within Europe, Great Britain can produce wheat more cheaply than can farmers on the Continent (again mainly a result of larger farms). West Germany, with small and fragmented farms, has the conditions that make cereal production uneconomic.

The degree and method of agricultural support is irrelevant to the argument. Whether farm prices are the result of producer subsidies (as in Great Britain) or high tariffs (as in the EEC) or are largely unprotected (as in Australia and New Zealand), the price paid to farmers must reflect the producers' costs plus the profits that are needed to induce the farmer to stay in agriculture. Obviously, consumer prices cannot be used for this purpose, since they reflect, in

addition to producers' efficiency, consumer taxes or subsidies and
the cost of transport, wholesaling, and retailing.

Even producer prices are not an accurate reflection of producers'
efficiency, insofar as they are affected by input subsidies—such as the
fertilizer subsidy in the United Kingdom and in some other countries—
but fortunately, for present purposes, these input subsidies are usually
much less important as a means of agricultural support than are output
subsidies—whether the latter are obtained (as traditionally in Great
Britain) by means of deficiency payments or (as on the Continent) by
means of import controls, both of which keep the price paid to the
farmer above what he would otherwise have obtained.

The input subsidies (production grants, including other grants
and subsidies not tied to the output of individual products—such as
drainage, water supply, and farm structure grants) of some £150 million, out of a total annual subsidy bill of some £270 million, paid to
farmers in the United Kingdom is rather larger than the input subsidies
to agriculture in other countries. For this reason, the producer price
criterion that has been adopted in this book may give an unduly favorable picture of British agriculture, but, in relation to the existing
differences between producer prices in Europe, it is not large. (It
represents some 5 per cent of a total net agricultural output of some
£3,000 million.)

There are two other factors that hamper the use of producer
prices as a criterion of a country's agricultural efficiency. One is
that cereals are, in all countries, the most important form of animal
feed; and high producer prices for meat, milk, butter, cheese, and
eggs may be a result of high prices paid by farmers for their purchases
of animal foodstuffs, rather than a result of their inability to produce
at lower prices.

If the concern is with the efficiency of agriculture as a whole in
any country, however, it is fair to say that high producer prices for
meat and dairy products, even if not a result of inefficiency on the
part of the producers of these products, are the result of inefficiency
on the part of another sector of that country's agriculture. This
argument is more difficult to sustain if, as in Great Britain and Denmark, imported animal foodstuffs are a large part of the total supply
of animal foodstuffs, but, in these circumstances, there is no obvious
reason why the prices of animal foodstuffs should be maintained at
a high level.

The second difficulty, a more intractable one, concerns rates of exchange. Obviously, the producer prices in the countries involved in any international comparison must be expressed in terms of a single currency and not in their national currencies—here, as in most international comparisons, they are expressed in dollars. Any devaluation of one currency in relation to the dollar will make the producer prices in the country that has devalued appear lower than they were before devaluation, although there has been no change in the productive efficiency of the farmers in the country that has devalued.

In 1967, Great Britain devalued by 14.3 per cent, New Zealand by 19.45 per cent, and Denmark by 7.9 per cent in relation to the dollar. Producer prices in these countries, when converted into dollars, were lower by these percentages after that year. There is no completely satisfactory answer to this problem, which also affects, for example, comparisons of national income and foreign trade expressed in dollars.

Two points can be made in defense of the producer price criterion of efficiency, however. Firstly, it can only be assumed (in all such conversions to a common currency) that the devaluations (or upward revaluations) that take place reflect underlying changes in the supply and demand position of the currencies concerned, and that the position after devaluation is something like equilibrium at that time, as is the position before devaluation. This presents a false picture if the years involved are those immediately before and after the devaluation, but a more accurate one if a series of years is taken. (Thus, price comparisons in the next section of the this chapter are made on the basis of the years 1965/66-1968/69.) Second, from the national policy standpoint, a devaluation (for example, by New Zealand) does mean that food can be imported to Great Britain from New Zealand that much more cheaply, and this factor should be taken into account by the British Government.

VARIATIONS IN AGRICULTURAL EFFICIENCY
IN EUROPE

Although the question has never been fully investigated, it is likely that variations in efficiency between countries will be larger in agriculture than in manufacturing. Capital and managerial and technical skills are mobile between countries, whereas land and climatic conditions obviously are not. Also, farming skills are probably more difficult to transmit to those countries that are backward in them, owing to the larger number of productive units compared with industry.

Even in those countries that have embarked on a course of building up domestic manufacturing behind tariff walls, there is some potential check on efficiency through the international mobility of capital and management. In agriculture, there is little check on efficiency through the mobility of factors of production, and the only practical check on efficiency is through international trade. In fact, in no country are agricultural imports free from some form of government control. For the same reasons, it seems likely that the potential gains from liberalization of trade in agriculture—in proportion to the volume of production and consumption—may be greater than those in manufacturing.

Large differences in productive efficiency are to be expected between countries with poor soil and climate—for example, the Middle East and North Africa—and countries with adequate rainfall and good soil. It is striking, however, that there are also very large differences in agricultural efficiency between countries with similar soil and climatic conditions—such as Western Europe (even if southern Italy, Spain, Portugal, and Greece are left out of the comparison because they possess less favorable natural conditions for temperate-zone agriculture).

Producer prices for the main agricultural products in Western Europe were compared in Tables I and 2. Because there are changes in the relative position of countries in single years, an average was taken of the last four years for which statistics were available. The same results as are obtained from a simple comparison of producer prices, translated into a common currency, should be obtained by measuring the margin of protection given to agricultural products in different countries. The margin of protection is the difference between the world market price and the domestic producer price.

For many agricultural products the concept of a world market price is rather nebulous, as there is no world free market; for many products, at least until recent years, the U.K. import price could have been regarded as the world market price, but many farm imports into the United Kingdom are now subject to minimum import prices, quotas, or some other form of restraint. Whether the base "world market price" that is being compared with domestic producer prices is or is not completely valid, however, the difference between internal producer prices and any common base price should indicate differences in the degree of protection to domestic producers afforded by the various governments and, at the same time, differences in productive efficiency.

Despite the great importance of this subject to governments that are (presumably) interested in the rationale of their own policies of protecting domestic agriculture, as well as in the potential gains from liberalizing agricultural trade, only one systematic investigation of the subject has ever been done. The results of this survey were published by the U.N. ECE in Economic Survey of Europe for 1960 and were reinterpreted by the late Professor E. F. Nash in 1962.[10] (See Table 28.) The only difference between the U.N. ECE figures and those of Nash is that the U.N. ECE adopted the rather confusing procedure of expressing protective margins as a percentage of domestic producer prices in each country; whereas Nash inverted the figures to show variations from a world market price base expressed as a percentage of that base.

The U.N. ECE survey covered the years 1956/57-1958/59 inclusive, and one would not expect there to be an exact correspondence with figures for a period ten years later. Nevertheless, the correspondence between Table 28 and Tables 2 and 3 is close enough to suggest that the results of the two studies are fairly accurate, and that Denmark has retained its position as the most efficient producer of most agricultural products despite the increasing difficulties that it has suffered from the development of the EEC CAP and the tightening of import restrictions in other foreign markets, including the United Kingdom.

The U.N. ECE figures show that, in 1956/57-1958/59, Danish producer prices of beef cattle, pigmeat, and eggs were below world market prices. The only other country in which this was the case was Ireland (for beef cattle, pigmeat, and barley). Irish producer prices for milk and sugar beet, however, were 90 per cent and 49 per cent, respectively, above the world market price, whereas the figures for Denmark for these two products were only 12 per cent and 14 per cent.

In the EEC and the United Kingdom, most domestic agricultural producer prices fell within a range of 30-100 per cent above the world market price—a similar, although slightly less favorable, relationship than the 20-100 per cent range seen in Tables 2 and 3 in relation to Danish prices—the only price falling significantly outside this range being the U.K. milk price, which was 203 per cent above the world market price.

VARIATIONS IN THE PRICE OF INPUTS

It was noted above that the criterion of producer prices as a measure of efficiency may be distorted by variations in the price of

TABLE 28

Agricultural Protective Margins, 1956/57–1958/59[a]
(Producer Prices As Per Cent of Base World Market Price)

Country	Milk	Beef Cattle	Pigmeat	Sugar Beet	Eggs	Wheat	Barley
Belgium–Luxembourg	127	30	2	36	44	67	16
France	61	26	—	15	5	18	10
West Germany	72	34	29	56	48	61	59
Italy	155	36	29	45	49	67	47
Netherlands	57	47	12	3	2	30	26
EEC (mean)	95	34	18	31	30	49	34
Denmark	12	X/32	X/15	14	X/22	18	0.5
Norway	165			—	33	89	25.0
Sweden	123	40	20	36	19	33	19.0
Ireland	90	X/31	X/35	49		16	X/33.0
United Kingdom	203			49	44	27	

[a] X = domestic producer price at or below the corresponding export price.

Source: E. F. Nash, "Agriculture and the Common Market," Journal of Agricultural Economics, XV, 1 (May, 1962).

producer inputs. This applies only to some inputs—particularly
fertilizers (which may be subsidized by the government, as in Great
Britain, or whose price may vary as a result of conditions quite outside
the influence of agriculture) and cereals used as animal foodstuffs
(whose price depends on the type and degree of agricultural support
used by the government with respect to cereals). The latter factor
gives the agricultural processors of animal foodstuffs (that is, the
milk, meat, eggs, and poultry sectors) an advantage in those countries—
mainly the United Kingdom—where producer prices are supported
mainly by subsidies, rather than by import levies or controls.

Variations in the price of labor are not relevant in comparing
producers' efficiency between countries; wages are better regarded
as a result, rather than a cause, of producers' efficiency. Thus,
although for example, wages paid to farm laborers in southern Italy
are lower than wages paid to laborers doing similar work in Great
Britain, this is not a threat to wages in Great Britain; low wages in
southern Italy are a result of low productive efficiency, and, if efficiency, increased, wages there would rise.

It may also be noted that better land and climate are not relevant
factors in considering the possible desirability of government intervention to support domestic agriculture. The only factors that are
relevant—in terms of requiring modifications to the producer price
criterion of efficiency—are variations in input prices that are themselves the result of government policy, that is, subsidized inputs (for
example, fertilizers) and the price of cereals.

From the price figures in Table 2, there is no reason to deduce
that the efficiency differential that Danish producers have in milk,
meat, eggs, and poultry is the result of being able to purchase cereals
as animal foodstuffs on more favorable terms. The main input that
is relevant here is barley, and the price differential for producers in
Denmark is less for this than for most of the "processed"farm products; in other words, the lower price at which Danish farmers are
able to sell milk, meat, eggs, and poultry is not attritutable primarily
to being able to obtain cheaper animal foodstuffs, but, rather, to
greater efficiency in processing, using the term to cover all the operations in meat, dairy, egg, and poultry farming. Conversely, lower
producer prices in Ireland, especially for milk and bacon pigs, may
be due, in part, to cheaper barley (and other feeding cereals, especially
oats, whose price is closely related to that of barley).

The producer price criterion, when adjusted to take account of
input subsidies, necessitates one major modification to the picture
of the relative efficiency of countries that emerges from the price

comparisons. It may give an unduly favorable picture of U.K. agriculture, due to the large proportion (about 50 per cent) of total farm support that is given in the form of price support. Although this may be
a large amount per unit of labor in agriculture, it is less significant
in relation to output and may, in fact, not be much out of line, expressed
per unit of output, with the input subsidies given by other governments,
including those of the EEC.

That producer prices for milk and beef are nearly 40 per cent
higher in Great Britain than in Denmark, despite input subsidies and
slightly cheaper animal foodstuffs, however, is an implicit criticism
of these branches of the industry and lends support to arguments that
have been put forward for a re-examination of government support to
milk production in Great Britain.[11] In this connection, it should not
be overlooked that there are now considerable potentialities for
international trade in liquid milk, as well as in butter and cheese.
Denmark has supplied milk by tanker to U.S. forces in Western Europe.
Imports of liquid milk into the United Kingdom have been almost
prohibited, ostensibly on health grounds.

In other products, particularly pigmeat, the efficiency differential
between Denmark and Great Britain has narrowed considerably. From
Table 28 it appears that, in 1956/57-1958/59, U.K. producer prices
for pigs were more than 35 per cent higher than Danish prices. (It is
not possible to say by how much more, since Danish prices are recorded
as being simply "less than world market prices" in the U.N. ECE study
of protective margins.) In the four years 1965/66-1968/69 U.K. producer prices for pigs, according to the IFAP figures (Tables 2 and 3),
were on average only some 4.5 per cent higher. The precise figure
here is not very significant, since pig breeding in Great Britain is
directed mainly to production of pork and in Denmark to bacon, but
the conclusion that the large efficiency differential in favor of the
Danish farmer in the late 1950's had been substantially reduced a
decade later is undoubtedly correct.

This conclusion is supported by a study of pig production costs
in Great Britain and Denmark made by the Farm Economics Branch
of the University of Cambridge, which concluded that "over the past
twelve years the difference between English and Danish costs per
score [20 lbs.] has fallen from 11s. 3d. to 4s. 4d." [12] (This latter
figure, which refers to 1963-65, implies that Danish costs were some
13 per cent lower than British at that date—33s. 3d. per score of pigmeat in Denmark compared with 37s. 7d. per score in Great Britain.)

NOTES

1. R. Dorfman, The Price System (Englewood Cliffs, N.J.: Prentice-Hall, 1964), p. 138.

2. Alan Gilpin, Dictionary of Economic Terms (London: Butterworth, 1966), p. 57.

3. R. W. S. Pryke, "Are the Nationalized Industries Becoming More Efficient?," Moorgate and Wall Street Review (Spring, 1970), pp. 55-72.

4. "For the national economy it can be assumed that the concepts of output at constant prices and real earnings evolve in a roughly parallel way notwithstanding differences due to foreign trade, investment and government consumption, etc. In other words, on this scale productivity may at a pinch be equated with average earnings per head. On the industry scale, however, it is no longer possible to assimilate the two concepts since average earnings per head evolve in approximately similar fashion in all industries, in keeping with the rise in national productivity, while the productivities of individual industries vary—often to a considerable extent."—from L. A. Vincent, in Productivity Measurement Review (May, 1961), put out by the Organization for European Economic Cooperation.

5. H. Jorring, Concepts of Productivity Measurement on a National Scale (Paris: OECD, 1965), pp. 36-37.

6. For example, E. F. Denison, Why Growth Rates Differ (Washington, D.C.: The Brookings Institute, 1968).

7. See FAO, The State of Food and Agriculture, 1968 (Rome, 1969), p. 78, graph of output per hectare of agricultural land and per active male; and FAO, The State of Food and Agriculture, 1963 (Rome, 1964).

8. The State of Food and Agriculture, 1963, p. 110.

9. International Wheat Council, World Wheat Statistics 1971 (London: International Wheat Council, 1971).

10. E. F. Nash, "Agriculture and the Common Market," Journal of Agricultural Economics, XV, 1 (May, 1962), 26-57.

11. Linda Whetstone, The Marketing of Milk, "Research Mono-
graph," No. 21 (London, Institute of Economic Affairs, 1970).

12. F. G. Sturrock and R. F. Ridgeon, "Pig Production: England
v. Denmark," Westminster Bank Review (February, 1967), pp. 57-63.

In the preceding chapters, the effect of the Common Market on world agriculture and also the attempts—mainly in EFTA and GATT— to deal with agricultural problems on an international scale have been examined. It is clear that the Common Market has had a substantial effect on the agricultural exports of third countries—an effect that has been mitigated or disguised by the rapid rise in consumption of many agricultural products, particularly cereals, within the Common Market.

Trade diversion must be regarded as a question of market shares as much as of trends in absolute exports, whether in tonnage or money terms. In a rational system, low-cost agricultural exporters could probably expect to have not merely a constant, but a rising, share of the market of the EEC and other major importing areas.* Guarantees on the basis of static export quantities or export receipts, such as appear to be Great Britain's aim in negotiations with the EEC, cannot be regarded as satisfactory. Still less can they be so regarded when, as in the case of New Zealand, the quantities are to decline and, in any case, appear to be guaranted only for the transition period.

---

*This is subject to the qualification that a rise in output in low- cost producing countries might lead to a rise in marginal costs and hence in prices, whereas a reduction in output in the high-cost impor- ting countries, such as the EEC and Japan, would fairly certainly lead to a reduction in costs and prices, since it would be the least efficient producers who left agriculture. Rising marginal costs in Australia, New Zealand, Canada, the United States, and Argentina, however, are a very long way off and may never materialize.

Figures of third-country exports to the EEC, if attention is devoted to market shares, show that the trade diversion effect of the CAP has been considerable for all agricultural commodity groups other than fruit and vegetables and for all animal foodstuffs other than cereals. All major exports from Denmark, and some exports from Eastern Europe, have suffered a fall not only in relative, but also in absolute, terms.

Although Denmark's difficulties will be resolved if Great Britain joins the Common Market, since it will regain some of its lost exports and, in addition, will benefit from higher EEC producer prices, most low-cost agricultural exporting third countries will then be in the same position as Denmark has been in since 1958. The effects of British entry into the EEC on world agricultural trade would be so far reaching, however, that few precise predictions can be made.

It has frequently been said both by British and Common Market official spokesmen that Great Britain must accept the principles of the CAP. This may simply mean that Great Britain must accept the machinery of the CAP. The essence of this machinery, although the details and terminology vary from product to product, is that imports from outside the EEC are charged a levy determined by the difference between internal producer prices and the world market price, the proceeds of which are used for internal price support, structural reform, and subsidies on agricultural exports to third countries. (The main method of price support in the EEC is, of course, the import levy system.)

The crucial question for Great Britain (as well as for third countries and for the efficient world allocation of resources) is not the machinery itself, but the level at which producer prices are fixed in the enlarged EEC and, hence, the size of the U.K. payments into the common agricultural fund, the size of the resulting U.K. balance-of-payments difficulties, and the size of the trade diversion effect on third countries. No useful prediction can be made of the effects—or the gains and losses either to the United Kingdom or to third countries—of British entry into the EEC until the level of producer prices within the enlarged EEC is known; it will not, however, be known until after Great Britain's entry.

There are many people and interests in both Great Britain and the EEC who would like internal producer prices to be fixed as low as possible and who hope for a gradual reduction in real and, if possible, in money terms during and after the transition period. Although the producer prices of a number of products in the EEC have been held constant and have thus experienced a decline in real terms (that is, after allowing for the effects of inflation), there has, in general, been no reduction of the gap between EEC producer prices and world prices in the years 1958-69, except in beef and veal, and, in some cases, including pigmeat and poultry, there has been a widening of the gap. (See Table 17.) On the basis of the development of the CAP to date, therefore, it is clear that the assumption that Great Britain can make the EEC an outward-looking unit, as far as agricultural trade is concerned, is by no means to be taken for granted.

The prospect of Great Britain's joining the EEC has brought to a head problems in world agricultural trade that have existed for a long time. During the years since 1958, there has been a tendency for high-cost agricultural exporting countries to increase their share of world exports, whereas the exports of the low-cost producing countries have remained static or have fallen. This trend has been evident in all the main temperate-zone agricultural products and has affected all the low-cost exporting countries.

If Great Britain joins the EEC, the trend is likely to be accelerated, since Great Britain is the largest food-importing country, unless there is a considerable reduction in internal EEC producer prices. There may also be less incentive for the high-cost producing countries in the EEC to rationalize their farm production and transfer farm labor to nonagricultural employment, since they will have a captive market in Great Britain. At the same time, as the largest food importer, Great Britain should be in a position to influence developments in the enlarged EEC.

Some reduction of the adverse effects of the CAP on Great Britain could be obtained by an expansion of agricultural production in the low-cost producing countries within the enlarged EEC—that is, Denmark, Ireland, and Great Britain. Although there have been efforts to expand agricultural production in Great Britain during the 1960's to meet the balance-of-payments problem, Great Britain has done little or nothing to raise its imports from Denmark and Ireland, measures that would have been prudent in anticipation of joining the EEC.

If the negotiations are successful and the transition period starts in 1973, it may not be possible to implement such measures after that date. In any case, it is clear that the contribution that could be made toward reducing the costs of entry to Great Britain in this way is small. In the longer run, the only solution can be by maintaining U.K. imports from non-European producers.

Any solution must involve coordinated international action. This is the element of truth in demands for international commodity agreements, either as a means of solving the problems connected with British entry into the EEC or for other reasons. In this, as in other matters, however, the establishment of new organizations and machinery is of no value unless there are criteria that can be used as a basis for action and, if possible, also a means of enforcement.

The principles on which action should be based have been set out in the preceding chapters. If import, export, or production quotas are enforced, they should be used to bring about a gradual reallocation of market shares in favor of low-cost producing countries. Average national producer prices can also be used to measure the degree of protection; and, as, in effect, has tended to happen in negotiations on industrial tariffs in GATT, the countries with the highest degree of agricultural protection can be required to make the largest cuts, not only in absolute, but in percentage, terms.

Most of the low-cost producing countries—New Zealand, Australia, Canada, the Union of South Africa, and South America—have embarked on a course of building up their own manufacturing behind high tariff walls. Although, in the existing situation, this is the only course open to them, since there is little or no prospect of expanding their agricultural exports, if measures were taken to allow their agricultural exports to increase, it would be logical to demand, as a quid pro quo, some reduction in their tariffs on manufactured goods.

Agricultural organizations in developed countries and also the governments of underdeveloped countries frequently say that GATT is not the right forum for discussing their problems, because of the principle of reciprocity (which is held by the latter to conflict with their presumed case for tariffs on infant industry grounds). It is apparently on the assumption that a substantial reduction or elimination of tariffs on imports of manufactured goods into underdeveloped and primary producing countries is not possible that proposals have been put forward for a North Atlantic Free Trade Area, excluding both these groups of countries.

If the assumption that reciprocity could be extended at least to the primary producing countries is correct (possibly with some flexibility and leniency regarding their existing tariffs, just as agricultural protection in industrial countries cannot be eliminated overnight), the case for forming a regional free trade area largely disappears, and the emphasis should be in strengthening GATT and accelerating the progress of GATT negotiations.

In GATT negotiations on industrial tariffs, the principle of "binding" tariffs on industrial goods—that is, of not allowing any increases—has been at least as important as the very substantial progress that has been made in tariff reduction. From the point of view of an exporting firm or country and in order to obtain the well-known advantages of international specialization, it is at least as important that an export market will not suddenly be eliminated by a tariff increase as that tariffs, in the long run, will be reduced.

The first step, therefore, should be to extend the principle of binding to agricultural protection, for which purpose the measure of protection used here—the difference between world market and domestic producer prices—could be adopted. In other words, agricultural policies of national governments should be operated in order to ensure that the gap between world market prices (or the export prices of low-cost producing countries, after allowing for any production or export subsidies) should not increase. If production costs and prices in low-cost producing countries fell, this would mean that prices in importing countries would have to be reduced if the degree of protection was not to increase.

These proposals—that degrees of protection (<u>montants de soutien</u>) should be bound and that they should be measured by the difference between domestic producer and world market prices—were put forward by the EEC negotiators in the Kennedy Round of negotiations in GATT. The United States objected to them, apparently on the grounds that binding agricultural protection would mean that high-protection countries would not reduce their degree of protection.

These technical objections should not detract from the fundamental importance and validity of the two proposals. It may be noted, however, that the proposal for binding agricultural protection is incompatible with the EEC levy system and, if adopted, would mean that the levy system had been abandoned. The essence of the levy system is that the procedure starts with fixing the internal producer price, and the degree of protection becomes whatever is needed to maintain that price.

For the same reason, it is very doubtful that the levy system is compatible with GATT, although, as usually happens when a powerful member insists on going its own way, GATT had to accept the proposals for the CAP when they were discussed in 1958-62. The degree of protection accorded to agriculture by the EEC, and in some commodities by Great Britain and the United States, is also fantastically high. In the industrial sphere, tariffs are now generally around 8-10 per cent, and a tariff of 20 per cent or more would be regarded as very high. EEC margins of agricultural protection in 1968-69 were generally between 150-200 per cent and, in butter, reached over 500 per cent. (See Table 16.)

PROSPECTS FOR A LIBERALIZATION
OF AGRICULTURAL TRADE

In the past, although the economic arguments for liberalizing international trade in agriculture have been recognized to be as compelling as those relating to manufactured goods, the political power of farmers' organizations, particularly in industrial importing countries, has been such as to block progress. Although this will remain a serious problem, there are several reasons why it should become more tractable.

First, as already mentioned, if Great Britain's application to join the Common Market in the early 1970's is successful, it is almost inevitable that there will be a worldwide reconsideration of international trade in agriculture and the machinery for dealing with it; and this is, in any case, likely to be insisted upon by the United States, as a major agricultural exporting country, in future tariff negotiations.

The changes in world agricultural trade arising from Great Britain's accession to the EEC would be so revolutionary and, if something like pre-existing EEC producer prices were maintained, so irrational that it is almost inconceivable that they could take effect without some offsetting action, probably taking the form of worldwide negotiations—in GATT or some other forum—covering the whole field of government policies toward agriculture and probably extending to international trade in both agricultural and industrial goods.

Second, a number of studies have tended to show that the most important reason for the difference between the high rate of growth in continental Western Europe and Japan, on the one hand, and Great Britain, on the other hand, has been the movement of labor from low-productivity occupations (mainly agriculture) in the former.[1] Although this does not suggest any way in which Great Britain's low growth rate can be improved, it does mean that high growth in the EEC and other Western European countries can be sustained and perhaps increased by a more rapid rate of movement of labor out of agriculture.

This is both desirable and practicable where the farm population is still large and the nonfarm sector of the economy is expanding rapidly, as in the EEC countries and Japan. The resulting problems for particular regions and the undesirably high rates of population growth of large cities, it is now generally recognized, should be dealt with by regional and urban planning policies, rather than by protecting agriculture.

Third, the decline of the farm population in the main consuming centers—Great Britain, the United States, and the six EEC nations— should make the political aspect of the problem more amenable. The farm population in Great Britain is now some 3 per cent and is still declining by about 3 per cent of the total per year. In the United States, it is 5 per cent. For the six EEC nations, the percentage of the population involved in agriculture was 29.2 per cent in 1951, 18.9 per cent in 1961, and 12 per cent in 1971;[2] it will reach the present U.S. figure during the 1980's and the present U.K. figure during the 1990's. (See, also, Table 29. There is a slight discrepancy between the figures in this table and those just cited above. The former shows the percentage of the working population involved in agriculture in 1950 at 28.8; the latter gives a figure of 29.2 for 1951. There is always some difficulty in producing a precise figure because of the number of farmers with some outside occupation and the number of farmers' families who work; also, before 1958, figures for the six EEC nations were particularly imprecise.)

Although experience in Great Britain and the United States shows that the influence of farm organizations does not necessarily decline as the proportion of the occupied population in farming diminishes, it may have this effect in the long run; and a decline as rapid as that in the EEC in recent years can hardly fail to affect the political balance. In addition, only a small proportion of farmers in the EEC are young (68.8 per cent are forty years old and over, and 34 per cent are sixty-five years old and over), so that generous pensions at the age of perhaps fifty or fifty-five for EEC farmers who wished to retire would go a long way toward solving the problem.[3]

A caveat should be entered here in connection with factors working toward a long-term solution. British entry into the EEC would ease the immediate problem of EEC farming, if there was a substantial reduction in imports from third countries or a rise in the price paid to third countries, to such an extent that economic pressure to rationalize EEC farming would be reduced.

TABLE 29

Percentage of Working Population Involved in Agriculture, 1950-65

Country	1950	1955	1960	1965
West Germany	24.7	18.5	13.8	11.0
France	28.3	25.0	20.7	17.0
Italy	41.0	36.1	30.8	24.7
Netherlands	14.1	12.2	10.4	7.9
Belgium	11.3	9.2	7.7	6.1
Luxembourg	23.9	20.2	16.4	13.5
EEC	28.8	24.1	19.6	15.9

Source: EEC Commission, Memorandum on the Reform of Agriculture in the European Economic Community, "COM (68) 1,000" (Brussels, 1968), Annex 2.

130

It seems, in fact, that there has been a slight fall in the rate of
decrease in the agricultural population in the six EEC nations during
the years 1965-70 compared with the preceding five years, which may
be related to the higher and more effective protection against imports
from third countries that was indicated by trade trends, the trend in
the gap between world market and EEC producer prices, and EEC
producer price trends in Chapter 2. Since Great Britain is a very
much larger net importer of food than are any of the existing members
of the EEC, the possible deleterious effects, in this as in other direc-
tions, would be large.

Finally, since the late 1960's, there has been, in almost every
country, a rapid acceleration of inflation, which many economists
hold to be cost rather than demand induced and, therefore, not amenable
to treatment by the traditional method of demand deflation. Despite
the vast amount of discussion of this question, the hard fact is that
the lines of action open to any government for dealing with cost
inflation are extremely limited.

One of the few policy measures that could bring about an immediate and substantial reduction in the rate of increase in the cost of
living is an increase in imports of food from low-cost producing
countries, and, if, as is possible, inflation becomes even more serious
and intractable in the next few years, it is difficult to believe that
governments will not make more use of this weapon.

Further economic research on two subjects is of crucial importance for economic policy formation regarding international trade in
agriculture. First, there is a need for a comprehensive forecast of
the world agriculture situation in, for example, 1976, 1980, and 1985—
based on different assumptions, with attention focused mainly on the
price gap between high-cost and low-cost agricultural producing
countries and how this is likely to change.

The real cost to Great Britain of the EEC CAP depends largely
on this gap. The gap (which is also a measure of efficiency and of
the degree of protection) would show the balance-of-payments cost—
through import levies or higher import prices—of not buying from
the cheapest source. The gap narrowed somewhat in the mid-1960's,
with the rise in world cereal prices, but has since widened again,
and the available evidence is that it is likely to continue to widen, or
at least not to narrow.

The inadequacy of research into relevant agricultural economic
problems during Great Britain's three attempts to join the Common

Market since 1960 has been remarked upon earlier in this book. No more urgent research subject from this point of view could be imagined than measuring and interpreting changes in the price and cost gap between high-cost and low-cost producing countries since 1950 or 1960 and predicting its likely course in the next decade or two, but hardly any research has been done on the subject.

The FAO, for example, has made detailed commodity studies projecting the likely world demand and supply situation for individual commodities up to 1975 and an "indicative plan for world agriculture" for 1985.[4] Other organizations and individuals have made similar projections. None of this research has included a forecast of the likely development of the price gap between low-cost and high-cost producing countries.

Second, the degree of protection for agriculture as a whole and for individual commodities in each country needs fuller investigation. A clear picture of the present situation is a vital precondition for reducing agricultural protection through multilateral bargaining. This book has adopted the simple measure of the difference between internal domestic and world market prices, which is the simplest measure and, in most cases, gives an accurate picture.

The modifications needed when input subsidies, not tied to any particular commodity, are taken into consideration should be quantified, as should some indirect subsidies to agriculture, including subsidies to rural electrification, which are given in all countries (including Great Britain, the United States, and the EEC), and items like relief from local rates and partial relief from estate duties (death duties) in the United Kingdom.

It is necessary to draw a fairly arbitrary line here, however, or no study would ever reach any conclusions—for example, public provision for agricultural education should probably be excluded. Once an accurate picture has been obtained of the degree of protection for each agricultural commodity, it is then desirable (although it has not been done here) to translate this into the degree of protection for agriculture as a whole, which involves estimating the degree of support to output or producers' incomes, rather than to unit prices.

From the data on producer prices used here, it appears that the EEC has a higher degree of agricultural protection than do the United Kingdom and the United States, and the producer price data also seem to indicate that the degree of protection in the EEC is increasing, whereas in Great Britain and the United States it is decreasing. The picture of Great Britain as a low-protection country is not altogether compatible with the picture emerging from the 1960 U.N. ECE study in Economic Survey of Europe for 1960, which suggests that Great Britain was a medium-protection country.

Also, a comprehensive study of agricultural protection in the EEC and the United States, undertaken on behalf of the EEC Commission and published in 1971, suggests that the degree of total protection of agriculture in the two is about the same.[5] The approach used was to estimate the effect of a total removal of all forms of agricultural support on the income of producers, and it was concluded that the effect would be to reduce producers' incomes by 50.4 per cent in the EEC and 44.3 per cent in the United States.[6] For individual commodities, the percentage by which income would be reduced was put at the following:

	United States	EEC
Wheat	56.5	47.2
Feed grains and rice	50.0	38.1
Meat		
Cattle	18.0	38.7
Pigmeat		23.2
Milk and milk products	4.5	64.6
Eggs and poultry (not protected)	-	15.2

According to these estimates, 73 per cent of total protection went to animal products in the EEC and only 35 per cent in the United States.

The degree of protection in the United States is much more difficult to estimate due to the variety of forms in which it is given, including import quotas, export subsidies, support buying, and subsidized domestic food programs. Also, estimating the long-run effect of removing protection on producers' incomes is a more difficult and hazardous operation than is estimating the immediate effect on prices of doing so, since it involves estimating the extent to which producers of highly protected products can switch to less-protected items, the extent to which they can increase their efficiency in both groups, and the effect on patterns of consumption. These problems cannot be cleared up without further study of the methodology of measuring degrees of agricultural protection, as well as the actual situation in different countries.

NOTES

1. See, for example, E. F. Denison, Why Growth Rates Differ (Washington, D.C.: The Brookings Institute, 1968).

2. EEC Commission, Evolutions et prévisions de la population active agricole, "Informations interns sur l'agriculture," No. 61 (Brussels, September, 1970), Annex A, Table 3.

3. Ibid., Table 4.

4. FAO, Provisional Indicative World Plan for Agricultural Development (2 vols.; Rome, 1970).

5. EEC Commission, Comparaison entre le soutien accordé à l'agriculture aux Etats-Unis et dans la Communauté, "Informations interns sur l'agriculture," No. 70 (Brussels, January, 1971).

6. Ibid., pp. 247-48.

Note: only the most important references to commodities and countries are listed.

FRANCIS KNOX, Lecturer in Economics at the Open University (Bletchley, England), holds a first-class honors degree in Economics and an M.Sc. in Urban and Regional Studies from the London School of Economics. He has taught at the University of Glasgow and the University of Leeds and has held economic research posts in the Economist Intelligence Unit, the National Farmers' Union, the Consumer Council, and the Board of Trade.

During the first series of negotiations between Great Britain and the EEC in 1961-63, he worked in the economics department of the National Farmers' Union, specializing in Common Market agriculture. He is thus one of the few economists outside the EEC who has been conversant with the development of the Common Agricultural Policy of the EEC since its inception.

He is the author of Consumers and the Economy, monographs on monopolies and restrictive practices, and numerous articles in economic periodicals and is currently working on a book on planning and economic development.

DATE DUE
